INSTA GRAM RULES

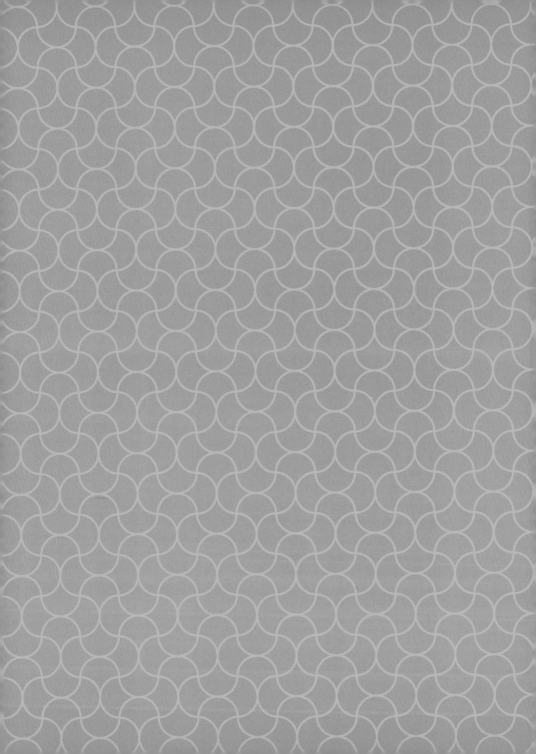

INSTA GRAM RULES

THE ESSENTIAL GUIDE TO BUILDING BRANDS, BUSINESS & COMMUNITY

JODIE COOK

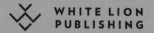
WHITE LION PUBLISHING

Contents

Introduction

There are Instagram accounts that are incredibly impressive. You've probably seen them. They pop up on your feed, their images are dazzling and their follower and engagement numbers grow effortlessly. They amass a tribe of superfans who rush to be the first to like an image or be the first comment. Their audience can't get enough of them. These accounts are responsible for the brand behind them, selling their products and building a vocal and committed community.

There are also millions of bad Instagram profiles out there, but the world needs (and wants) those that shine bright and stand out. It needs the ones people rave about to their friends and revisit over and over again. It needs those remarkable accounts to learn from, look up to and champion.

The book you now hold in your hands invites you to join them.

The people behind incredible Instagram accounts are organised and prolific. There's no escaping that. They have systems and processes and they relentlessly learn and experiment. What these accounts have in common with yours is that they too started with zero followers and zero images. After that, it's expertise, application and determination, supported by a great product or cause.

Herein lies the knowledge, the plan and the inspiration to replicate their methods and create your Instagram success.

So who am I to be telling you this? Well, I've been a social media professional since 2011. Organisations from niche start-ups to global stars and everything in between have relied on my guidance to make social media a key driver of their growth; growth in sales, influence and databases. I regularly contribute opinions on current social media affairs for international publications and I have built a team of remarkable social media managers, trainers and consultants who manage, train and teach our methods.

The digital agency I run guides Instagram accounts from zero to hero based on the principles and practices you see laid out here. My team creates plans from scratch, manages the process on behalf of busy companies, consults with marketers and spots the small improvements that, when combined, make a huge difference. We've agonised over algorithms and cheered for campaigns. We've seen the patterns behind success.

Like you, I'm a student of social media; always learning, testing and working out how I can grow the brands of my clients by applying commercial thinking to social media activity.

The 125 rules are here to give you an actionable framework from which to operate. The eight contributor profiles bring the rules to life, provide inspiration and remind you that it's all possible. When reading the contributor profiles, see what strikes you about their stories. Although few say it directly, it's clear that much of their Instagram success lies in consistency and enthusiasm.

Behind every great Instagram brand is a solid product offering. This 'product' could be digital or physical, it could be a service provided by you or your team. The product could be a cause for change or for educational or entertainment purposes. It could be your personal brand. The substance of this product is the foundation upon which the guidance contained in this book will work from.

Throughout the book, I'll guide you through every aspect of Instagram success, split by strategy, content, community and growth.

Strategy is where we ascertain how Instagram sits within your marketing plan, creates goals and determines what success looks like. Content is for giving ideas and developing systems for creating and sharing brilliant content, including ways you won't have previously considered. Community is where you become noticed, then invaluable, to your audience. The focus of growth is ramping up everything achieved so far and taking your account to the next level. There's a final bonus section, health, to ensure you run your Instagram, not the other way around.

I recommend reading a few of the rules at a time, then pausing to apply them to your Instagram account. Keep a notebook alongside you. If a specific rule doesn't fit with your account, just move on to the next, but stay open minded and ready to learn. Base your actions on feedback from your own community and results from your own account, rather than second-guessing or sticking to what's expected. Aim to stand out rather than blend in.

Instagram often trials new features before rolling out the best to all its users, of which 500 million use the platform every day. It's likely that the future holds enhanced analytics, closer integrations with shopping platforms and more ways of serving and interacting with a community. However, the premise and the basics of the platform remain the same. Instagram wants brands, influencers and consumers alike to spend more time using it, so every evolution of the platform serves this goal.

Whilst I can't predict every impending Instagram change, I can recommend that you jump straight on new features and be ready to experiment with commercial awareness in mind. Be prepared for any new feature to pivot your strategy, if it matches your brand and voice and is well received. You can find out about new features first by following @InstagramForBusiness on Instagram.

At any point, any of the features mentioned within this book could be removed from the platform, for which I can only apologise. Nevertheless, the premise of each feature holds true: look for ways to serve a community, look for methods to add value and look for excuses to engage.

Your audience is waiting to hear from you. If you're proud of your product then it's ready to meet more people and here's how you do just that. Let's begin.

Chapter One
Strategic Approach

The first section of this book is dedicated to optimising your Instagram account for long-term success. With a strong foundation, you can build a formidable Instagram presence and a brand that is synonymous with what you stand for.

Your account and everything it shares must contribute to the bigger picture. So you need to be clear on what that bigger picture is and create an account that will get you there. For this, you need a strategy.

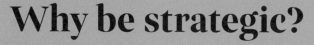

Why be strategic?

A strategic approach is hugely important if you're taking your Instagram presence seriously because it provides a framework to work within. Knowing what your brand represents and where you want to go makes your social media activity a more conscious endeavour and allows you to push your online activity further.

By 'strategy', I don't mean specific tactics for quick wins but laying the groundwork for long-term success – from setting the right profile picture to choosing the right filters. It should be an embodiment of your entire Instagram presence and what you want your account to achieve for your personal brand or business.

Benchmarking where you are now against where you want to be is paramount: you might not realise how far your account has come until you look back. Growth in likes, followers and comments will become the norm, but applying the tactics and reflecting on them regularly will ensure this continues.

Of course, it is possible to grow an Instagram account without a strategy, but not while trying to maximise the chances of growth. You'll see from the case studies included throughout that even those Instagram accounts that started off without a plan, or with a scattergun approach, had to adopt a strategy at some point on their journey.

Without considering your account's identity, it's easy to be busy on the platform without being productive or effective. A strategy keeps you on track, and if things aren't going well, you at least have an understanding of what you've been doing so that you can change it.

The four steps to building an effective strategy

This chapter is split into the following four areas:

1. Goal-setting
2. Profile Optimisation
3. Brand and Branding
4. Tone of Voice

These elements flow on from one another and combine to provide the foundations for success.

Goal-setting

This defines the purpose of your account, allowing you to identify the direction you want to take.

Profile Optimisation

With your goals in mind, you can now optimise your profile. This is about how you define yourself, attract the right audience and showcase your brand.

Brand and Branding

Your brand and branding is the way everything looks and feels to users. The strength of your brand underpins how you're perceived online.

Tone of Voice

This is the way you 'speak' or 'sound' on Instagram. This is an integral piece of your identity because the way you communicate is still highly important on the platform, even if most of your content is based around imagery.

Goal-setting

Almost every article or book about achieving success will discuss the importance of goals, and Instagram is no different. Goals will define your strategic approach; they will help determine your plan during the coming weeks and months, and help you decide what content to post. They may also dictate how you set up your account and how it operates. Goals are where it all begins.

Knowing where you want to go is not always a prerequisite to moving in the right direction, but it does help, preventing you from becoming completely lost or going the really long way round. Time-bound goals also give you a way of measuring the rate of your progress, which can be benchmarked against your previous performance or that of similar accounts or competitors. Your account might be growing, but is it growing faster now than it was a month ago? Is it growing faster than your closest competitor?

Aside from the practical benefits of having a set of goals to work towards, the actual process of putting goals in place makes you think carefully about what really matters to you. It makes you consider the role Instagram plays and could play in the success of your brand. Success is unique to everyone, and unless you've identified it, how do you know if you've reached it?

Once your goals are set, they are a great way to assess your progress and monitor success. When you have goals and timelines in place, you can decide what's working, what's not, and how you may need to shift your approach. This dynamism and flexibility is only afforded when you actually have a record of your efforts and achievements.

Creating and tracking your goals will give your Instagram strategy cohesion, consistency and authenticity. It will help keep you in line and on track, even when things might not be going to plan. In fact, being able to shift strategy and create new ideas while working to the same goals are valuable skills.

Developing goals

Create separate and distinct goals for the short, medium and long term to help clarify what you want to achieve at each stage and stay on track.

THE LONG TERM: PAINT THE PICTURE

Project your thinking into the future. Where are you, what are you doing and what does your day-to-day life look like? What does success look like for your future self? You can write it down, you can draw it, you can even make a vision board.

Now think about the Instagram account of this future version of you. What does it look like? How many followers do you have? What do you post about? What kind of people are you engaging with? How much time do you spend on Instagram? What kind of comments do you receive on your posts and stories?

SHORT AND MEDIUM TERM: ASK THE QUESTIONS

Now you can start to think about the smaller, more manageable goals that will get you to this place.

RELATIVE VALUES

Bear in mind the role Instagram plays in your life and how it serves you from a commercial perspective. Not everything you do on the platform needs to make money, but it must work towards bringing you value, even if that's only in the long run. Distractions online and in your business will tempt you away from your task, so it is important to avoid anything that doesn't contribute to your goals.

EVOLVING GOALS

Goals will always be a work in progress. Goal-setting is a skill that you can hone and you should revisit this section over time to reassess your goals and develop new ones. Your goals will evolve – some might simply have been too ambitious; others too conservative – and you may have completely different ambitions to those you started out with. If your goals don't change, it could be a sign that you're not developing or that you're just not achieving them for one reason or another.

Consider the following questions and add your own, to help set your short- or medium-term goals.

- ◄ How many posts can you create within the next month?
- ◄ What's your follower goal for the end of this year?
- ◄ Which three people do you trust, whose feedback you can ask for?
- ◄ How many new ideas can you think of each month?
- ◄ How can you change the demographics of your followers?

START DRAFTING YOUR GOALS

1 Set three audacious goals for the long term.
  Think big. Make them almost unbelievable in their
  scale and ambition. Write them down.

2 Create up to six medium-term goals that will be achieved
  over a shorter period of time, the results of which feed
  into the three ambitious goals you have just made.

3 Think about four or five goals you can achieve over
  the next month. Make them smaller, more focused,
  and ensure they feed into the medium-term goals
  you created.

The following seven actionable rules will help you develop
meaningful short-, medium- and long-term goals for your
Instagram account. Take them all on board and think about
how you can apply them to your unique situation.

FOCUS ON YOU

During your time on Instagram you will see many
others doing their own thing in order to achieve their
own goals. It is easy to start imitating – you might not
even realise you're doing it – but having your own clear,
defined goals will prevent you getting sidetracked by
others. Use other Instagram pages for inspiration, but
have the confidence to persevere with the plan you
have created that is unique to your brand.

1. Test each goal

Now you're equipped with an idea, however vague, of what you want to achieve over the short, medium and long term, it's time to test the goals.

It is crucial to believe in each goal you create for yourself. You need to want it and be prepared to put in the short- and medium-term actions in order to achieve it. Arbitrary goals – those that you don't really believe in or can't see a path to achieving – will most likely remain unachieved.

Think about each of the goals you have created and ask yourself *why* you want to achieve it. It might be:

- ◂ a specific follower number because that fits with your version of what makes a successful account

- ◂ a specific engagement rate because that's what will make you feel like your followers are listening and interested

- ◂ a specific look and feel to your account because you want your Instagram feed to match the colour scheme and look of your branding

- ◂ a specific number of enquiries each month because that's what will generate a certain amount of revenue.

Your goals might be in place because they fit with your own version of success, someone else's version of success, because you're benchmarking against similar accounts, or you simply want to achieve certain revenue goals. Each of these responses are fine, but make sure there is a reason. If you don't know why you want to achieve something, replace it with a different goal.

Split your goals into those you have complete control over and those you have less control over. Try to make 80 per cent of your goals those that you can fully control.

YOU HAVE COMPLETE CONTROL OVER:

- ◀ how much you post
- ◀ what time you post
- ◀ the type of content you post
- ◀ how many people you follow and who they are
- ◀ how many reach-outs you make
- ◀ how much you engage with other accounts
- ◀ how quickly you respond to comments
- ◀ how fast you implement new Instagram features.

YOU HAVE LESS CONTROL OVER:

- ◀ your follower or engagement numbers
- ◀ who approaches you for opportunities
- ◀ how many enquiries or messages you receive
- ◀ people's opinions of your content
- ◀ how many comments you receive and how positive they are.

2. Create goal checkpoints

Once you have decided on your goals, assign goal checkpoints.

At each of these checkpoints you will assess your progress towards your goals and make any required amendments. You might realise you're smashing your targets and need to extend them. You might decide to rein some in or give them a different priority weighting. I recommend a goal checkpoint every quarter, so set one three months from now.

Organising your goal checkpoints in this way will mean that all of your energy on Instagram goes into the *inputs*. You'll be so focused on creating and taking action that the goals you have set will be secondary. It might even be a nice surprise when you check your progress every three months and realise how far you have come; checking daily just won't have the same effect.

When assessing how you're achieving your goals, it's important to take a step back and look at the overall trends. It might be tempting to assess your goals every day and measure your success on the last thing you posted, but remember that it takes time to build an audience and create relationships. It takes time for them to understand you and your brand. It will certainly take time to grow your account to the stage where posts achieve a certain number of likes or comments.

In any given day there will be fluctuations in your account and your follower numbers. Post reactions and account popularity can go up and down, even by the minute. This is a marathon, not a sprint!

3. Set time goals

Avoiding a boom and bust strategy in favour of sustainable, consistent actions will set you up for success. Spending hours on Instagram over two days then ignoring it for the rest of the week isn't what growing accounts are made of.

Part of your goal-setting involves defining the amount of time you want to spend on the platform each day or each week. Make a schedule of actions to ensure you know what's coming up and what you need to do at each frequency. A schedule like the one below might help you.

	Morning (15 minutes)	Afternoon (10 minutes)	Evening (20 minutes)
Monday	Post story	Follow accounts	Post image. Measure week and assess profile.
Tuesday	Ask question	Respond to comments	Hashtag research and next week's content planning
Wednesday	Post story	Outreach to target audience	Post video
Thursday	Post story feature	Post image group	Unfollow accounts
Friday	Post story	Respond to comments	Post image
Saturday	Add to story highlights	Outreach to target audience	Post story and schedule video for tomorrow
Sunday	INSTAGRAM-FREE DAY		

Don't be restricted by these suggestions! Start with a blank piece of paper and create your own unique schedule that works for you; one that operates around your other commitments and takes into account your short-, medium- and long-term goals.

4. Prioritise the metrics you want to achieve

Now it's time to prioritise your goals. Trying to fulfil multiple agendas won't be as effective as putting your goals in order, planning your actions and smashing them one at a time.

Some goals are achieved at the detriment of others. For example, if your goal is to post engaging stories and continue conversations with followers via direct message, it might come at the detriment of a goal to only spend 10 minutes per day on Instagram. You might also face trade-offs concerning quality and quantity, or how niche your content can be before it compromises how much you can post.

Decide on the most important metric to you right now and put that one first when considering your short-term actions. Achieving that goal might serve to make the rest more attainable when it's their turn to be number one priority.

THAT'S RIDICULOUS!

In order to enter an Instagram competition posted by a brand as part of a collaboration with its partner, I had to follow two accounts, like the post, tag a friend in the comments and subscribe to a newsletter from a bio link.

The complex and unnecessary requirements of the competition – optimising for followers, likes, engagement and subscribers – meant the main goal of competition entries was unfulfilled (it achieved zero entries), despite the prize being very impressive.

THREE THINGS TO CONSIDER

1 If you were looking at your account from a completely fresh perspective, what's the one thing that, if it were improved, would ensure a better first impression?

2 Trust your instincts. What does your instinct tell you that you should focus on first?

3 Are there events in the future that you can time certain goals to coincide with? For example, a public-speaking opportunity might be a chance to achieve your follower-number goal, while the lead-up to that could be used to tick off your profile optimisation goal.

5. Benchmark against other accounts

Standing still on Instagram is not an option. It means making no progress, not learning from your activity to date and not making the most of new features. In fact, standing still, effectively, means going backwards because you'll be overtaken by others making better use of features and growing their accounts and influence.

There are no limits to engagement numbers, follower numbers and opportunities opened by achieving the goals you have set for yourself. If other accounts are achieving better outputs with the same inputs, they're doing something differently that you can work out and emulate; their success will provide valuable learning opportunities.

If a company or person with a similar market to yours is achieving certain outcomes, take inspiration, but find your own style, as that's what makes your account unique and attractive to your audience. Goals based on other accounts serve as moving goals, ensuring you don't become complacent with your account once it hits a certain level.

ONE METRIC TO COMPARE: ENGAGEMENT RATE
1 Identify an account that represents where you want yours to be and look at their last five posts.

2 Work out their like:follower ratio by dividing the number of likes on a single post by the number of their followers.

3 Work out their percentage engagement rate by multiplying that number by 100.

4 Do the same for your own account.

5 Compare the two and set an engagement rate goal for your account.

6. What's plan B? Plan C?

Look at your list of goals. Now imagine that your plan A doesn't go as envisaged and you aren't achieving the goals. What's plan B and plan C? Make a record of these plans, too.

Some of the best Instagram accounts didn't set out with specific commercial or metric goals in mind. Their main goal? To have fun. To be creative, to enjoy themselves, to be true to their values and post whatever they felt like posting. They didn't set any stall by metrics, so when the followers, likes and comments came flooding in, it was a nice surprise.

This way of operating isn't as effective as making a plan and being consistent and intentional about growing a successful Instagram account. There might be multiple ways of achieving the same goal, so if plan A doesn't work then it's on to plan B and plan C.

If, after a sustained period of time, what you're putting out there isn't having the desired effect, it's time to revisit. It's not giving up and it's not admitting defeat, it's just changing tack. Successful Instagrammers are adapting and hanging in there when all others have given up.

Consider an Instagram account that posts product images of T-shirts printed in California, with the goal of selling T-shirts. The account isn't successful in selling T-shirts, so it shelves plan A (selling T-shirts by sharing pictures of T-shirts) and moves on to plan B (selling T-shirts by promoting California).

The account starts posting images of Californian beaches, towns, sunsets and people and the account grows. The growth means that more people check out the profile to see what the account is about and they go through to the website and start buying T-shirts.

7. Outline your strategy for achieving each goal

A goal without a strategy is just a wish and wishing doesn't equate to Instagram success.

Each short-, medium- and long-term goal you have created requires a plan to take you from where you are now to where you want to be, having achieved it. It includes the actions and tactics you will employ to get there.

Your first strategy should be to learn more about how to achieve each goal, seeking clarity on the day-to-day actions that will take you there.

LEARNING METRICS STRATEGY

- Identify the gaps in your knowledge and find resources to fill them.

- Approach popular Instagrammers and ask them about how they achieved their Instagram goals and what they are.

- Schedule learning checkpoints at three-month intervals to explore new features and how you can make the most of them.

Now create a different strategy for each goal.

CONTENT QUALITY STRATEGY

- ◄ Identify and define the look and feel of posted content, including filters.
- ◄ Research content tips and tricks, including cameras, and implement any relevant ones.
- ◄ Set future checkpoints to assess the feed quality and make edits.

CONTENT QUANTITY STRATEGY

- ◄ Block out content creation and content posting times in calendar.
- ◄ Set reminders to post.
- ◄ Allow content planning time.
- ◄ Research scheduling tools.

ENGAGEMENT METRICS STRATEGY

- ◄ Plan consistent learning. Dissect every post that has gone badly and every post that has gone well.
- ◄ Research typical engagement rates and compare each post to them.
- ◄ Actively attract engagement by changing the captions and active outreach to audience members.

FOLLOWER METRICS STRATEGY

- ◄ Schedule follower number checkpoints or make a spreadsheet to record and track any changes.
- ◄ Research how best to gain new followers and employ tactics in order of feasibility and relevancy to your account.

Papier, UK
@PAPIER

Holly Chapman, Head of community

The stationery brand immersed in its community of stationery addicts.

Papier's followers are united by a love of stationery, design and expressing themselves through pen and paper. The account started in 2015 when the company was formed and has grown to over 196,000 followers. We hear Papier's strategy behind the growth of their brand and Instagram account.

WHAT ARE YOUR GOALS ON INSTAGRAM?

At the start our goals were to show our range of designs and reach a bigger community of stationery fans outside our existing customers. Now, it's about connecting with our community and our followers engaging with our brand. We aim to provide inspiration for our audience, build our brand awareness online and offer an additional presence outside the Papier shopping experience.

When Papier started, we didn't have a content strategy for our Instagram account, so it was a little haphazard in its look and feel. Since then, we are better at creating content tailored for the channel and now we feel it's quite distinctive and reflective of the brand - colourful, joyful and stationery heavy.

HOW HAVE SALES GROWN AS YOUR COMMUNITY HAS GROWN?

We see a direct correlation between the size of our community, awareness of the brand and as a result, a growth in sales. Revenue from Instagram grew 115 per cent in January 2020 when compared to January 2019.

We track sales and report on them on a monthly basis. We can also see repeat orders from customers acquired through our Instagram via our analytics tool. The data helps us to identify what's trending with our customers and to get instant feedback about new designs or collections.

HOW DO YOU ENGAGE WITH YOUR COMMUNITY?

We find that stories are a great way to ask questions and gather opinions. We have a community of ambassadors who regularly post our latest collections and we get many shares on stories of Papier deliveries from our customers too. Our followers have created some amazing content, especially with their new diaries, which encourages people to post and share their Papier purchases too!

Through Instagram, we offer exclusive previews of upcoming design collaborations and behind-the-scenes content to get to know our community of artists, designers and brands better, which often have an overwhelming response. Our artists and brand partners often join in with our conversations or do takeovers on our channel, content which results in high engagement.

WHAT DO YOU DO EACH WEEK?

The Papier brand voice is friendly, fun, informative and with a few hints of French. We don't want to take ourselves too seriously, so make sure that all of our copy, whether on social media or email, is light-hearted and uplifting. We try to avoid being too prescriptive. Apart from our ads, we tend not to boost or promote our organic content. We believe organic and paid content have different goals.

We aim to post a grid picture every day as we have so many exciting things to talk about from new collaborations to content from our online magazine, to our products and what we're doing behind-the-scenes. We incorporate a wide variety of images into our profile, from those made in-house to pictures taken by our customers and ambassadors, and illustrations by our team and artists. Our audience likes to see Papier being used in different ways.

Now we know our customers and what they like. We know that colourful, floral or romantic assets are more successful than muted colours or images that don't look 'real world' enough. We analyse what does well and we try to create new content based on that.

We try to keep our messaging consistent so we plan our posts in advance, in line with our other brand activity. For stories we post three or four times a week to talk about news and other exciting activities going on at Papier in more detail.

We get the most engagement early in the morning, at 7am on weekdays and around 9am on weekends. We see a big increase in our account after a lot of community outreach and relationship building.

WHAT ABOUT HASHTAGS AND THE INSTAGRAM ALGORITHM?

We are not the biggest hashtag fans! We use them only if they're relevant to special days or occasions (eg. #mothersday), otherwise we keep them to a minimum. We encourage all our customers and followers to use #lovepapier so we can see what they're posting and naturally, we support the community of #stationeryaddicts on Instagram.

We have found that the algorithm changes regularly and quickly so it's best not to create a whole strategy around it. The change made to the ordering of the feed (from recency to relevancy) has challenged brands like ours to be more creative with the content.

WE AIM TO PROVIDE
INSPIRATION FOR OUR
AUDIENCE, BUILD OUR
BRAND AWARENESS
ONLINE AND OFFER AN
ADDITIONAL PRESENCE
OUTSIDE THE PAPIER
SHOPPING EXPERIENCE.

WE TRY TO KEEP OUR
MESSAGING CONSISTENT
SO WE PLAN OUR POSTS
IN ADVANCE IN LINE
WITH OUR OTHER
BRAND ACTIVITY.

Profile Optimisation

Your Instagram profile is the keystone of your presence on the platform, providing viewers with an overview of who you are, what you do and what your business is, so optimisation should be a top priority. How well your profile is set up will determine your success in achieving the goals you've outlined. It should inform, inspire and signpost. And the best profiles do this effectively and efficiently, perfectly combining form with function.

There are three types of Instagram account. The default is the personal account, which is the one most users on the platform have. The second type is the business account, the best option for virtually all commercial entities or organisations. The third and most recent addition is the 'creator' account. This was specifically designed with the influencer in mind, whose business is essentially content creation.

There are benefits to all the different accounts, so select the right one for you.

The key components of all Instagram profiles include:
- profile picture
- name
- bio
- number of followers
- number of accounts you follow
- profile stories
- link
- home feed.

To follow or not to follow?

Your profile is the nucleus of your Instagram account. When a new user visits your profile they decide whether or not to follow you. Therefore, the first job of a profile is to ensure it appeals to your target audience, rather than the broadest audience possible. Your profile can manage people's expectations when it comes to the nature of the content you'll share and who it is meant to appeal to. After that, your content will be what enables you to reach new audiences and influence their following, interacting or buying decisions.

Users have several options when it comes to taking action on a profile. Each user will explore your profile in a different way and follow a unique journey. They can:

- follow (or unfollow, if they're already following)
- send a private message (DM)
- read the bio
- click on the profile link
- scroll the posts
- click and interact with images
- view your profile stories
- visit the shop
- view the tagged posts.

It's plausible that their first exposure to your Instagram account will be through a post rather than your profile, but the profile is where a new or prospective follower will head if they're interested in the account. Your existing followers are also likely to return to your profile from time to time.

Profiles are the most static part of the platform, yet your profile will never be completely 'finished' and a complete overhaul may be required now and again. However, it's important that you operate within the best practices when it comes to profile optimisation and the brand that you create.

The following nine rules show the ways in which we can optimise the elements of the profile in order to create the best possible user experience.

1. Use a list format in your bio

Your Instagram bio is there to explain who you are in a clear, succinct way, to help people decide whether your account is one they might want to follow. Use the 150 characters available to:

- ✦ introduce yourself
- ✦ describe yourself or your account
- ✦ share your mission
- ✦ signpost the type of content followers will see
- ✦ indicate why someone might want to follow you.

This is a large amount of information to fit in quite a small space, so list formats are very popular with Instagram users. They're quicker and easier to understand than lines of text, and often represent a better and more efficient way of providing information.

If your brand has a simple strapline, use this as the first line of your bio, then add the list. Include four to six bullet points, depending on how long each one is. Don't feel the need to use every single character you're allowed; sometimes brevity is more powerful and effective.

WRITING THE PERFECT BIO LIST

- ✦ Prioritise key elements by placing them at the top of the list.
- ✦ Make each point clear and appealing.
- ✦ Use keywords that people may search within your niche.
- ✦ Avoid too much jargon or anything that could be misunderstood.
- ✦ Use emojis or other design features in place of bullet points, to help elements stand out.

2. Add story highlights to your profile

Instagram story highlights are collections of Instagram stories that feature permanently on your profile. Story highlights appear prominently, between the bio and the posts. They change the appearance of your profile significantly. Without them, your bio link and the 'followed by' section below continue straight on into your feed posts.

Unlike normal Instagram stories, which remain on your profile for 24 hours, stories added to highlights are visible permanently by anyone viewing your profile. A story highlight can contain up to 100 stories, so there's plenty of opportunity to have some fun with them.

Profile stories add context to your brand, segment elements of your presence and aren't as perfectly polished as feed posts. Think of them as a behind-the-scenes; a chance to grab attention and engage with followers in a different and more personal way.

HOW TO USE INSTAGRAM STORY HIGHLIGHTS
Each story highlight should cover a specific topic and be titled accordingly. These can include separate elements of your brand, such as 'events', 'customer reviews' or 'about us'. Stories help visitors understand your brand and business.

Optimise your profile by designing covers for each of your story highlights, matching your brand guidelines. A cover is an image you upload that crops to a circle when displayed. You can use an existing story post to create a story highlight cover, or the default highlight cover will be the first story in the highlight.

Keep adding to your stories with your best content in each category and remove anything within them that is outdated or doesn't represent you well.

You should have at least four story highlights to ensure your profile looks complete, but as many as seven will be seen on the desktop before users must scroll right to see all of them.

3. Use emojis to add colour and personality

Using emojis in Instagram bios makes a profile more interesting and unique. The account's theme and topics can be gleaned at a glance and someone can quickly see if they have similar interests to you.

SEE FOR YOURSELF
If you saw these emojis in an Instagram bio, you would know very quickly what the account was about:

Emojis can be used as the bullet points in your bio list, as decoration, or as a way to add more information without literally spelling something out. They convey messages very succinctly while adding personality.

USE EMOJIS TO:
- convey personality following a written sentence
- provide additional information without taking up valuable characters, for example a country flag emoji to show your current location
- as bullet points themselves (try stars or right-facing arrows)
- highlight key information, placing hearts or arrows around a particular word or phrase
- give more context to bullet points, for example an award you won might be introduced in your bio using the medal emoji.

Choose relevant emojis to represent your brand or organisation and keep these consistent throughout your account; your profile's emoji use should reflect how you intend to use them in your content. If in doubt, don't overdo it; think quality over quantity.

4. Choose your profile bio link wisely

Your bio link is part of your strategic approach. With a compelling profile and a large follower base, it's likely to attract a reasonable amount of traffic, so use it wisely.

Other social media platforms allow you to add links to every post you publish and every comment you make. However, on Instagram most accounts can only link to other sites in the bio and in direct messages. Links included in captions and comments won't be clickable, and they can't be copied and pasted.

WHERE SHOULD I LINK TO?
Use your bio link to direct users to:

- ⊿ your own website
- ⊿ a website designed specifically to offer several link options on a single page, such as Linktree or Link In Bio
- ⊿ a specific landing or signup page
- ⊿ another social media profile, for example LinkedIn
- ⊿ your profile elsewhere, such as an author page on Amazon
- ⊿ your shop page elsewhere, perhaps Etsy or eBay or Amazon.

It should be clear, either from the link itself or an explainer at the end of your bio, where the link will take users.

TRACKING

An advanced use of this link is to use a tracking link. Or to link to a version of your normal website that has been optimised for Instagram users. Ninety-nine per cent of the traffic to this link will be from a mobile, so make sure it's mobile responsive and optimised.

5. Match your bio to your other social media accounts

Profile optimisation means consistency across all the platforms on which you have a presence.

Having congruous social media profiles unifies your brand. Your profiles will differ slightly due to the discrepancies and nuances of each platform and you may well have different goals for each platform. However, if someone comes across your Instagram account they should be able to identify you from your Twitter or Facebook profiles, and vice-versa.

FOUR WAYS TO ENSURE CONSISTENCY

1. Where possible, have matching usernames across platforms.

2. Use identical or very similar profile pictures across your social networks and choose the same information for your bio. If you opt for emojis, use the same ones for each platform.

3. Change the order of information in each bio so it's relevant to how you use the platform. Consider an education lawyer working in Chicago with a side-business of custom cake-making. Twitter might be about education law, while Instagram might be about the cakes, so ensure the bio reflects both components in a different order.

4. Even if you aren't particularly active on other platforms, make the profiles and bios look good and use your profile to direct people to Instagram, signposting that your Instagram account is the one you update most frequently.

Ensuring your suite of social media profiles work together is a key component of your strategic approach.

6. Security and account settings

Review your account settings regularly, to ensure you're displaying the right information to the right people.

SECURITY SETTINGS

- ◀ Is your account private or public? If private, people need to request to follow you, and your content, bio, followers and followings are only displayed to those you accept. A public account is best, unless there's a specific reason for it to be private.

- ◀ You can choose to provide contact details for your account. If your account is a business profile, you could give an email address or phone number.

- ◀ People can comment on your posts unless you have comments disabled. Comments are usually welcomed, but you can change this if there's a specific reason to do so.

- ◀ Set filters for comments, so that those containing profanities are automatically hidden.

ACCOUNT AND NOTIFICATION SETTINGS

- ◀ Enable two-factor authentication for additional protection against unauthorised use of your accounts.

- ◀ See how much time you've spent on Instagram, to check it's within your time goals and assess how productive that time has been.

- ◀ Control the push notifications and how many emails you receive. Opt to turn all push notifications off to ensure your Instagram activity is deliberate and intentional and can't interrupt your other work.

- ◀ There are also several miscellaneous features of Instagram, including location settings, dark mode, language settings and accessing the data that Instagram holds on you.

7. Create the ultimate profile picture and username

Make your username as clear and simple as possible and ensure your profile picture best represents you or your brand.

PROFILE PICTURE
Your profile picture is your visual representation on the platform and it accompanies your account and its content wherever you go. On Instagram, it will be shown as a small circle, so make sure it does your brand justice.

For a personal account, follow these rules:

◀ Use a picture of your face in the style of a headshot.

◀ If your account is smiley and happy, smile! If your account is serious, change your expression accordingly.

◀ Save full-length images and pictures with other people for your feed and story images. This one is about you.

◀ Set aside some time to take some profile pictures and keep going until you find one you're happy with.

◀ Ensure both the background and image are as clear as possible. Use portrait mode on your phone to fuzz it further, or hire a professional photographer.

For a brand account, follow these rules:

◀ Use a square version of your company logo, which works when displayed as a circle.

◀ Ensure it is readable, even when reduced to a mobile screen.

◀ Avoid the temptation to show group shots or product pictures here, unless the product is instantly recognisable and close up.

USERNAME

Your username is equally important, and it is displayed to your followers in the feed. Unlike Twitter and Facebook, where your full name is displayed with your posts, on Instagram your username is the only thing that shows next to your posts.

You have 30 characters available for your Instagram username, but try to use fewer than 15. If your own name or brand name is available, use that. If not, you can be clever about how you use full stops and underscores to recreate the name.

- Use an underscore (or two) between your first and last names.
- Use a full stop between your first and last names.
- Start the username with 'iam' followed by your full name.
- Use a title prefix, so Mrs, Mr, Dr, Ms.
- If you have a degree, use MA, BA, BSC and so on, after your name.
- I have seen some accounts use the word 'the' before their name.
- Use an underscore after your name, but not a full stop.

If you've identified an account with the username you want and it's dormant, consider reaching out. The person who owns it might be happy to let it go or sell it on.

8. Unfollow unnecessary accounts

The Instagram accounts you follow form part of your online presence. You'll be associated with the accounts you follow and your account is likely to be suggested to others based on this information, too.

WHAT DOES WHO YOU FOLLOW SAY ABOUT YOU?
You can get a good impression of someone from who they follow on Instagram. Political leaders or parties, bands, celebrities and news sources all paint a picture of their personality and interests.

LET'S TALK NUMBERS
The number of accounts you follow is shown prominently alongside how many followers your account has. The ratio between these numbers is key. An account with 10,000 followers that follows 12,000 is far less impressive than one that only follows 500.

MINIMISING THE NOISE
The content of every account you follow will populate your news feed. Minimising the amount of irrelevant content will help you stay on top of the accounts that really matter to you.

NEXT STEPS
Go through all the accounts you follow and unfollow the most random and irrelevant. Ask the following questions:

- What does following this account say about me?
- Do I want to see this content in my Instagram feed?
- Would I miss this account if I didn't follow it?
- Is this account sharing information I could get elsewhere (e.g. if you already follow them on a different platform)?

If you're unsure, keep following the account and move on to the definite unfollows. See how much of a difference it makes to your numbers and the quality of your news feed.

Use this process every few weeks. Going forward, think carefully before following any new accounts.

9. Verify your account

Being verified means that Instagram has confirmed your account is the authentic presence of the public figure, celebrity or global brand it represents. It gives you a little blue tick next to your name and makes your account look super professional. It also makes your account easier to find when someone is searching for you and ensures you appear more prominently in relevant searches.

To submit your account for verification, use the 'request verification' option within Instagram. You will be asked for proof of your identity, so you can upload your driver's licence, passport, or official company documents if it's an account for your brand.

Instagram's main motivator for verifying an account is if it's felt that it is genuinely plausible that there might be confusion between a 'famous' person's or brand's account and others of a similar name or description. The same applies to accounts that are believed to be significant enough to be imitated. Instagram offers some guidance on what they take into consideration, namely that your account is authentic, unique, complete and notable.

For now, anyone can submit their account to be verified once every 30 days. Instagram will let you know via a platform notification whether you have been successful or unsuccessful. Don't be disheartened if you are not accepted for verification. It doesn't mean you're not authentic or notable and plenty of large and successful accounts don't have that blue tick.

Brand and Branding

A strong, well-conceived brand identity will facilitate your account growth and your Instagram goals. Users set a lot of store by the way a brand presents itself, making decisions about its stature, commitment to quality, who its customers are and even its political or ethical views.

How you go about defining and creating your brand is up to you; it should be unique to you, your business and your sector. Ultimately, you must develop a brand that someone in your audience will want to align themselves with. Luxury and performance brands, especially, play on the fact that fans or users like to feel they adopt some of the qualities that your brand stands for. You should leverage this power, too.

Having a great brand is largely down to attention to detail and not cutting corners. Spend some time optimising your profile and maintain a strong sense of brand throughout everything you share. This is where serious Instagram users differentiate themselves. You must be prepared to design your brand, create guidelines and stick to them religiously.

Brand guidelines

Brands should have extensive guidelines that they enforce for their internal designs and for anyone looking to use brand assets such as their logo. Serious brands are fiercely protective of their branding, to ensure consistency and that nothing looks odd or out of context. Consistency screams professionalism and a commitment to delivering products or a service that meets expectations, every time.

The reason people visit the same restaurant or coffee shop chains over and over is because they know the experience they're going to get. Familiarity is an incredibly potent influencer. People learn to trust brands; they associate the name, logo and colours with experiences.

Developing your brand

Branding is big business. Branding consultants and agencies are in high demand because of the importance of how brands are perceived, from building relationships with audiences right through to making the sale. Major brands go through full rebrands every few years to ensure they keep up with trends and reflect how their business has evolved. Rebrands are seriously costly when you consider changes across digital and print media, as well as signage and uniform, where applicable. Nevertheless, time and time again, companies decide it's worth it.

Developing or redeveloping your brand will be your primary focus here. It's important that you are completely happy with your brand and that it reflects your organisation's ethos and offering. Your brand will convey your values whether you intend it to or not. Appreciating how it comes across to other people is very difficult, so research and feedback are important in this phase.

Feeds can look very professional if everything's on brand, and this is largely down to the use of colour and tone; these are very important as they transcend your profile and your content. On the following pages are eight rules that focus on developing a visually compelling brand for Instagram and show how to adhere to it moving forwards.

1. Decide what defines you

The best Instagram accounts operate within a niche, such as health and fitness, lifestyle, travel, sport, fashion, automotive, business and entrepreneurship, beauty, music and animals.

CHOOSE YOUR NICHE
1. Decide on your main niche or theme. In which area are you an expert or influencer?

2. Decide on your sub-niches or themes (one or two maximum).

3. Use this to dictate the future content you post and how your bio is laid out.

Often, individuals will follow you because you post about a certain sport, fashion or technology, for example. Posts too far outside of this theme risk alienating followers unless they've totally bought in to your account or you as a person. It's the same with your brand; it should generally suit one particular niche or interest area, making it clear that's what the majority of your content focuses on.

BEYOND NICHE

An account can assume different roles within those niche areas. Are you a cool content generator or an expert offering insights and commentary? Will you be evidence- and fact-based or more opinionated? Maybe you won't be saying very much at all and you're going to let your images and videos do the talking. All these elements will have implications for the design and feel of your brand. Use emojis, key terms and the style of the brand to make users feel at home.

2. Align yourself with similar brands

Brands similar to yours can be a sterling source of guidance and inspiration, whether in shaping your brand or just gleaning ideas of how you can apply your own brand to an Instagram profile.

Look for the brands that you know appeal to your audience members. They may be direct competitors, synergistic brands or those who operate in a similar space. Pay particular attention to those accounts that have adapted their brand specifically for Instagram and utilised all the features with bespoke designs or content. When you see an account doing this well, it's impressive. It speaks volumes about their attention to detail and their professionalism.

Once you've done some research, you can choose to adopt similar styles, with your own spin or twist. Also take note of things that you don't like and know to avoid these moving forward.

Specifically look out for:
- ◀ use of colours and text
- ◀ how they theme or lay out their feed posts
- ◀ what they do with their daily stories
- ◀ how they utilise story highlights
- ◀ how their name, bio and link work together.

Shortlist four or five brands you particularly like and take screenshots of their profiles, so you have them to hand for inspiration and can keep an eye on any changes.

3. Choosing your palette

The colours you use have the largest effect on the overall feel of your account. Your key colour should match the logo of your brand or the main colours of your website. Ensure there is a crossover with the colours of your products or other elements of your business or brand.

Colours have different popular connotations. Red is seen as passionate, ambitious or dangerous. Green is eco-friendly, healthy and progressive. Some associate dark blue with authority, trust and luxury. Keep these in mind, and opt for something in line with your own values and goals.

Define up to four main brand colours. From these, decide on your single dominant colour, the one that people instantly associate with your brand. Then choose one secondary colour that is not as prominent but that is present in your logo or designs. This should be significantly different to your primary colour but must be complementary. Experiment with a few different combinations and get some feedback. It's important that all the colours you choose work together in all possible combinations.

Create your palette and keep it handy. You can do this using an online palette generator. Make a note of the RGB or HEX codes for your chosen colours.

Naturally, your primary colours will dictate how you brand your profile, but your palette also informs the colours and shades you incorporate into your content. Your entire profile should ooze your brand colours and what they stand for.

BRANDS ASSOCIATED WITH SPECIFIC COLOURS
You might not even need to see the name of the company to know which brand these colours represent. That's how powerful your colour palette can be.

Deliveroo: turquoise and purple
Amazon: black and yellow
Apple: white and silver
Cadbury: purple

4. Match brand and colours across all of your online presence

Extending beyond Instagram, ensure that your branding is used throughout your online presence, including your website. Social networks such as Facebook, Twitter and LinkedIn all have profile banner images, which provide space for branding.

If you are able to, use a graphic designer to apply your brand and colours to all of your social media profiles. They'll be able to create images in the correct format and dimensions. Alternatively, there are online tools available which can modify images to fit each of the major platforms' requirements, providing a quick and free option to achieve this. When using these, make sure you double check how each profile looks after each round of changes.

Small differences in the visuals of different social profiles are totally acceptable, because something that works for Instagram might be off the mark for LinkedIn, for example. However, it should be obvious at a glance that each social media profile you maintain for yourself or your brand is part of the same collection, with the same goals and ethos.

Your brand colours play a key role in recalling and recognising your brand. Every time someone comes across your brand online, it's an opportunity to reaffirm your branding.

5. Archive old posts that no longer fit your brand

It's easy to post something that you think works in the moment, but on reflection you realise it's no longer representative of your brand and the message you want to give out.

Scroll back to the first thing you ever posted on Instagram. Starting here, look through all of your content and archive (rather than delete) posts you're no longer happy with or that just don't suit your brand.

Reasons to archive old posts might include:

- ◀ off-topic subject matter
- ◀ low-quality imagery
- ◀ wrong colour
- ◀ off-brand caption
- ◀ contains mistakes or outdated information
- ◀ poor relative performance (low number of likes).

Archiving posts doesn't delete them forever and you can add them back to your feed at a later date if you want to. However, it does hide them from view and reduce the number of posts displayed in your profile. Improving your follower to post ratio is another benefit of doing this as accruing a large following from a smaller number of posts is more impressive.

It's natural for a brand to evolve over time and it's likely that the quality of your content will have progressed since you first began using Instagram. Erase everything that's not up to scratch.

6. Ask someone to describe your brand to you

It's impossible to have a 'first impression' of an account you've spent hours honing; you simply cannot have a completely objective view of your brand, your account and how it might be perceived by a stranger. You're just too close to it. Yet this is crucial in securing new followers and growing your influence.

Recruit the help of other people. Trusted friends, colleagues or family members will be able to give you invaluable feedback. Finding individuals in your target market elevates the value of their feedback, especially those you trust, who have your best interests at heart and who will give you their honest opinion.

Ask a friend to ask someone they know to check out your Instagram account and tell you what they think. They'll be far more forthcoming with their thoughts if they don't know you personally.

Ask for answers to the following questions:
- ◀ What kind of person buys from this brand?
- ◀ Is this brand high-end or low-end? Why?
- ◀ What do you think of how this brand is presented?
- ◀ What values does this brand have?

Ask several people for feedback. Don't rely on just one or two people, whose opinions might not be shared with everyone else. You'll almost certainly be surprised by some of the comments you receive. Ideally, you'll find some trends and a general consensus to inform your decisions and actions going forward.

7. Consistency of brand and message

Many businesses and organisations rely on their brand to help them resonate with their audience, make them instantly recognisable and serve as a beacon of their virtues. When brand consistency isn't there, all of these things can become lost or confused.

Take your key brand designs, styles and messaging and convey them strongly across all your social media platforms and any websites or other materials you share. This includes your real-life place of work, if applicable. Use one of your social accounts or your website as the foundation from which all your other accounts are based.

TOP TIP Guard your brand fiercely and never compromise the quality of a social media post or shared piece of information for speed. Keep your standards high.

Individuals access the internet from all kinds of devices, and every social network renders differently on mobile devices, especially as they're often accessed via an app rather than a web browser. Investigate your Instagram and other social channels from a range of devices to see how they appear and make changes as required. Ensure your key brand features and messages pull through, regardless of screen size.

Many profile designs are crafted on large screens and may have text or detail that simply doesn't render well on smaller devices. Use the largest file size possible for each post.

ADVANCED STEPS
Each social network has its own typeface, but on Instagram you can use different fonts in your bio if you wish. To incorporate other fonts and font formats into your Instagram bio and captions, you can use the following:

- igfonts.io
- apps4lifehost.com/Instagram/CaptionMaker
- influencermarketinghub.com/free-instagram-fonts-generator

8. Create brand guidelines

Use the concepts and rules decided upon so far to create your own set of brand guidelines. This document becomes a workbook for your online presence and can be shared with anyone who acts on your account.

If you choose to outsource or get help with your social media presence, the document should form the basis of any activity. The document itself doesn't have to be complex and fancy. It simply needs to contain all the basic details in terms of colours, typefaces and how your logo should be presented. It should also contain guidance on your tone of voice and content.

How to create a simple brand guidelines document:

- Create a new Word or PowerPoint document, beginning with your brand name, social handles and strapline.
- On a new page, add your logo in various file types and sizes – usually a light on dark background and dark on light background version. It's usually worth having a greyscale version and a clear background (.eps) version.
- Include guidance on how your logo should be used and oriented and the minimum clearance required around it.
- On a new page, show and define your colours, including your palette and when each colour is used.
- Include your approved typefaces for headings and body copy, plus links to download the font files.
- Use a new page to outline key adjectives that describe your brand.
- Include individual pages that answer questions such as 'This brand stands for . . .'; 'This brand loves these words . . .'; 'This brand doesn't say/do these things . . .'.
- Add guidelines specifically relating to Instagram, including a page for 'Instagram post guidelines', including the format, filters, captions and hashtag requirements of every post sent from your account.
- Include a page for Instagram stories, including the font, layout, colours and design that should always be used for stories on your account.

Tikiboo Fitness, UK
@TIKIBOOFITNESS

Kayleigh O'Connor, Marketing manager

The funky activewear brand using Instagram to secure repeat custom.

Tikiboo Fitness launched in May 2014 and the Instagram account opened six months later. The team's goal for Instagram was to gauge interest in the brand and its products. Now their goal is to engage customers further and grow Tikiboo's online community in order to reach more prospective customers.

Their focus on engagement with customers has meant that Tikiboo's customer return rate is high. The brand now has 41,100 Instagram followers, many of whom are superfans. Here, Kayleigh shares insights into the Instagram strategy.

TELL ME ABOUT THE ACTIVITIES YOU CARRY OUT ON INSTAGRAM

We post on our Instagram story seven times per day, and although we don't have a consistent rule for feed post frequency, we try to add something daily and at different times of the day in order to engage with a range of different users.

We place much of our effort on maintaining high-quality photography. We find making our images and videos visually appealing and aligned with our brand helps engagement and page growth and helps us to develop a pool of well-engaged users who we can remarket to. If we are launching something brand new, we know the post will do well. However, we also know that photography, model and theme choice have a part to play.

We used to post everything on our main Instagram account but this made it difficult to keep a consistent look on our feed, so we set up @styledbytikiboo to reshare customer content and run a monthly competition whereby we encourage our community to post images of themselves in our products. We also use this channel to ask community-focused questions, run polls and play Instagram story games.

Across our team we proactively find and engage with new accounts in order to grow the community. We also try to respond to every Instagram message we receive or every story we are tagged in, but this is near impossible!

Now we know that Instagram can be used for a variety of strategies, we use it to build relationships with new and existing customers, in order to increase the customer lifetime value. We share more user-generated content than ever before and we use our Instagram grid to tell a visual story, so that like a homepage, once you land there you get an immediate feel for the brand.

CAN YOU TELL ME ABOUT YOUR COMMUNITY?

Our community is mainly female runners in their thirties or older, who are supportive and fabulous! As well as our two Instagram accounts we have a Facebook community of over 11,000 members. We use our Instagram and Facebook pages to direct people towards this community group, as we find that the word-of-mouth marketing within that group is our strongest asset.

We have a brand document that we developed with the help of our Facebook community group. We worked together to understand which books, TV shows, people and products our community associate themselves with. This has heavily supported our return customer rate, which stands at 74 per cent. Most of our customers get the Tikiboo-bug and want to collect as many patterns and prints as they can.

ARE YOU ABLE TO TRACK SALES AND REPEAT BUSINESS FROM INSTAGRAM?

We track network referrals and can see sales attributed to specific platforms via Shopify, but it's difficult to comprehend exactly how much custom comes from Instagram. We can track sales from the Instagram accounts of our affiliates because they have unique codes, and our 'shop my instagram' tagging on our @styledbytikiboo account helps tracking, too.

Focusing on our community has helped to maintain and grow our channel, which ensures we can rely on return custom. We focus on relationships, not just reach, to reap the benefits of audience loyalty and continual engagement from our followers. The Instagram algorithm wants us to have a conversation with our community, and this is why user-generated content is only growing in importance.

TALK TO US ABOUT HASHTAGS AND PAID PROMOTIONS

Hashtag research isn't something we spend a lot of time on, but we often test different hashtags. We use Facebook Ads Manager to promote our content, but only for product launches and competitions.

HAS YOUR ACCOUNT GROWN FASTER AT CERTAIN POINTS AND, IF SO, WHY?

Yes. During competitions where we have asked people to follow us in order to enter, and when we have collaborated with big brands on our prints. For example, we saw a large increase of followers when we launched our Sesame Street collection, our dogs collection and our charity collections.

Similarly, when we have worked with certain ambassadors, who are not necessarily celebrity status, but who are well-connected individuals in specific areas (i.e. Clubbercise instructors), we notice an increase in followers.

MONDAY

IT'S LIKE THAT PERSON
THAT SHOWED UP TO THE
PARTY UNINVITED

I MEAN YOU ALLOW IT
BUT HOW RUDE!

TIKIBOO

WE POST ON OUR
INSTAGRAM STORY SEVEN
TIMES PER DAY, AND
ALTHOUGH WE DON'T
HAVE A CONSISTENT
RULE FOR FEED POST
FREQUENCY, WE TRY TO
ADD SOMETHING DAILY.

WEBSITE:
WE USE COOKIES
TO IMPROVE
PERFORMANCE

ME: SAME

TIKIBOO

WE SHARE MORE USER-
GENERATED CONTENT
THAN EVER BEFORE AND WE
USE OUR INSTAGRAM GRID
TO TELL A VISUAL STORY,
SO THAT LIKE A HOMEPAGE,
ONCE YOU LAND THERE
YOU GET AN IMMEDIATE
FEEL FOR THE BRAND.

Tone of Voice

The tone of voice of your account is how you deliver your content through captions, direct messages and comments. Even on Instagram, where images reign supreme and transcend language and cultural differences, words play a fundamental role in your approach.

The tone and language of your Instagram account is the closest thing it has to a personality. People follow accounts for unique and relevant content, perhaps for the latest news or offers, and while visual content is obviously hugely important, they also want to stay in contact; to 'hear' from the account regularly.

The nature of delivery has huge implications for the way the words are received. They can add humour, additional interest or make reference to other accounts, places or previous posts. Captions provide valuable context for posts, elevating or completely changing their purpose and meaning. They are also key in making connections and encouraging actions in audience members.

Aligning tone of voice and brand

The tone of voice of your account is closely linked to your brand because it affects how it is received and understood by your audience. Brands and businesses take their voice seriously. They align themselves with ambassadors that share that voice and in adverts they select voiceover artists and actors that reflect their brand perfectly. Your Instagram account must find the voice that helps define its personality. This is another key element in building familiarity and trust with an audience.

Often, audiences feel a connection with a brand because of the way it speaks to them and it's key that they feel this connection is authentic. Whether knowingly or not, audiences prize authenticity above almost everything.

It's not that someone would feel they're being deceived, but there is an element of investment in an account that a lack of authenticity could undermine.

Inconsistencies in language represent a telltale sign that an account is being managed by more than one individual, which can make users feel like the account is not a priority in a brand's marketing plan, or that it's part of a marketing engine. If your account is being managed by a single person, it's important that shines through, and consistency is pretty much the only way it can be achieved. If it's being managed by multiple people, they must all adhere to strict voice, tone and language guidelines.

Crafting your voice

One of the challenges we face on social media is that we don't actually have a physical voice when writing copy. This means that everything we need to get across must be right there in the letters, characters, emojis and spaces on the screen. Conveying humour, sarcasm, inflections and other techniques available to us in speech is simply not possible. So being smart and accurate with your wording is key to getting your message over.

With the introduction of video, it is possible to have an actual voice, music and sounds on some posts and the nature of these must also be considered.

This section provides seven actionable rules to craft your voice to support your brand and account goals. Use the advice given in conjunction with content-related rules in order to combine great imagery with compelling captions.

1. Mind-map adjectives to describe your brand's tone of voice

Take out a paper and pen. Write down key words or phrases that define your brand. From each of them, branch out and write related adjectives and other words that describe your tone of voice and personality.

Think about famous people that your brand should sound like. Having a specific person in mind helps you embody the tone as you post.

A tone of voice is multi-dimensional, conveying your purpose and a range of emotions. Here are some dimensions to consider:

- ◀ How funny is your account? What kind of humour?
- ◀ Busy/hectic or calm?
- ◀ Intelligent and expert or curious and openly learning? Or a mix?
- ◀ Loud and brash or quiet and timid?
- ◀ Intimidating or approachable?
- ◀ Likeable or an acquired taste?

FOR EXAMPLE:

- ◀ A healthy meal delivery brand, with the voice of: approachable, knowledgeable and efficient. This builds out into no-nonsense language and captioning that conveys their commitment to speed and service.

- ◀ A luxury candle and fragrance brand, with the voice of: soothing, relaxing and calming. This builds out into long and luxurious wording that focuses on getting people to slow down and be present.

- ◀ A professional graphic designer, with the voice of: quirky, attentive and creative. This builds out into unique insights, seeing normal things in new ways and ensuring others understand the thought process and the eye for detail that goes into their work.

2. Decide on your style and vocabulary

Next, work on how that voice and the adjectives that describe it are delivered on Instagram. An upbeat and friendly voice could use short, monosyllabic sentences, or long, complex ones with an academic vocabulary.

Your tone of voice is shaped by the words and language you use as well as the style in which you use them. Everyone has their favourite words and phrases and you should adopt a style you're happy with. This is reflected in your bio, captions and how you interact with other accounts.

Some questions to answer:

◄ How does your account address other users? By their Instagram handle? First name only? 'Bro'? 'Honey'? 'Mate'? 'Guys'?

◄ What about greetings? A formal 'Good morning' or 'Hey!'?

◄ Does the account use kisses ('x's) as a signoff?

◄ How directly do you answer queries?

◄ What about emojis? Which ones, how often and when?

It might seem obvious to you how your account 'speaks', but create some rules and guidance anyway. This keeps you in check and also helps if other people are managing the account. Refer back to your brand guidelines document and add a page to cover writing style and vocabulary. Include the following:

◄ words used to address people

◄ phrases used to greet

◄ responses to compliments

◄ responses to negative comments

◄ approved emojis to be used.

3. Compile a blacklist of words and phrases

A brand isn't just defined by the things it says; it's also defined by the things it doesn't say.

Define your brand and differentiate yourself by avoiding words and phrases used by other accounts in your niche. Think about your brand as if it were a person. What should it avoid saying? Which topics would feel alien to your values and ethos? If you believe a certain phrase dumbs down your brand, portrays it negatively or puts a spin on the account that you don't like, add it to a blacklist.

This blacklist should form part of your brand and style guidelines and can contain words, phrases, hashtags or even entire topics of conversation. When compiling the list, offer alternatives for the words or phrases you want to avoid.

- ◀ Never say 'Happy Friday' to end the week, or make any reference to Friday being a superior day because that's not how your audience of aspirational entrepreneurs view the week. Instead, say something about how productive the week's been and how you're going to smash next week.

- ◀ No talk of politics or the weather because your audience is international and has a range of political beliefs. Sporting events are fine as long as you speak about the event itself without picking teams.

- ◀ Never use sad emojis in any way because you want your account to radiate positivity and uplift your audience. No to the crying face, the poop or any sad faces.

4. Consistency = familiarity = trust and comfort

Consistency of language is paramount on Instagram, sometimes even more so than the visual elements.

Updates from your account should be welcomed like a best friend onto the feeds of your audience, but it only takes a couple of rogue words to disconcert them and upset that rapport. Pay attention to how you write and 'sound' every time you post.

TOP TIP When writing captions, write for the audience. Too many captions are written for the writer, not the reader.

Spelling, grammar and punctuation also play an important role, since misspellings signal lack of care and attention or give away that someone else is posting on your account. Get your grammar knowledge perfected and follow the same rules each time you post.

IDENTIFYING INCONSISTENCIES

Go through your last 20 posts and find any that don't fit the description of your voice or the style you've now outlined. Highlight why that's the case and make a note to ensure that your account conforms to all your guidelines moving forward. This rule is especially important for those accounts that have a very distinctive style and voice because changes will stand out dramatically.

5. Consistency of emojis

Emojis are a constant source of debate. Some people love them, others despise them. We've already seen that they can add a colourful dimension to your bio, and this goes for your content, comments and other communications, too. Emojis form part of the day-to-day language for many Instagram accounts. So just like traditional written text, be consistent with their use.

Given that they're so appealing to the eye, it's very easy to lose your way when it comes to emojis. Identify a range of emojis that your brand uses and stick to those.

Bear in mind the following rules.

◀ Don't use the same emoji to represent different things.

◀ Make sure the ones you use render properly for everyone.

◀ Don't try to convey too much with emojis as they can be misconstrued.

◀ Use them to add humour and context or to say something very obvious.

◀ Set a maximum number to use per update or comment.

◀ Create an emoji blacklist, just as you have a phrase or greeting blacklist.

If you want to opt out of using emojis all together, that's fine too.

6. Create a mood board

A mood board serves as a visual representation of your tone of voice and content and embodies your style and ideas. Choose images that align with your brand colours and feel. This means they'll be much more useful to you when composing your own content, too.

This is also a good opportunity to tie-in any images shared by brands you aspire to or want to align with. Bringing the best images from a selection of accounts into your mood board helps you absorb their influence without copying anything from a single post or feed.

Your mood board can include:

◀ your colour palette
◀ the fonts and graphics you like to include in your posts
◀ patterns, borders, outlines that match your brand
◀ a visual representation of the audience you're speaking to, including mantras they believe in, what their home looks like and how they might dress
◀ posts or stories shared by other accounts.

Create a digital mood board on a private Pinterest board. Pinterest acts as a comprehensive search engine for images and has the functionality to store the ones you like in one place, where you can see them all at the same time. You can even take screenshots of other Instagram accounts and add them as pins.

Alternatively, get out the glue sticks and printed images and make a physical mood board, perhaps one that hangs above your desk and reminds you of your brand, tone, voice and messaging.

7. Who are you talking to?

To help shape your voice and message, imagine you're addressing someone specific on Instagram. Who exactly is your account communicating with? How would you speak to them in real life?

Think about:
- what kind of person they are
- what they find funny
- who they admire and take inspiration from
- who they look to emulate in their actions
- their hopes and dreams
- their pains and insecurities
- how they live, including their daily routine.

Identify an individual who totally embodies the traits and thoughts of your target audience. This could be someone you've already met, already know of, or someone well known (which will help if there are two of you working on the account). Keeping them in mind when communicating will reinforce your choice of language and tone.

INTENTIONALLY CONNECTING

Get intentional about communicating with your target audience. Everything you share should be written for them in order to inspire a reaction and influence their thoughts or actions. This tactic helps you better empathise with your audience and choose your wording more thoughtfully. Going too broad is a mistake, while trying to resonate with everyone might mean you resonate with no one.

You'd speak very differently to a 19-year-old university student than you would to a senior law firm executive. You'd speak differently to a typical reader of the *Sunday Times* than you would a reader of the *Sun*. For maximum effect, define a specific member of your audience and speak to them how they want to be spoken to.

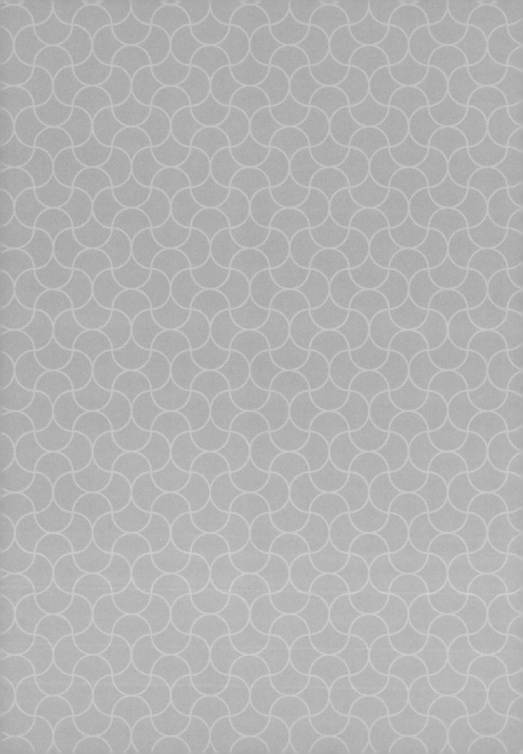

Chapter Two
Content

The content shared by an Instagram account defines its presence and underpins its success on the platform. A perfectly optimised account with a brilliant strategy goes nowhere without great content. This chapter will equip you to improve the content you already share and provide inspiration for a broader range.

In a sense, your content represents your Instagram profile's marketing campaign. The volume of high-quality content you distribute determines the reach and influence of your account.

Why does content matter so much?

Instagram is a content platform. How individuals and brands communicate, at least to their followers and audience en masse, is through the content they share and the success of that content plays a role in reaching new audiences.

With a defined strategic approach and a strong sense of brand and tone of voice, your content is now the main tool with which to achieve your goals. For businesses, content requires far more thought than it does for a personal account. But while a random, unplanned, spontaneous approach can work for some individuals, a more systematic approach will maximise your chances of success.

When we discuss 'content', we're looking at:

◂ image posts
◂ videos
◂ image/video collections
◂ Instagram stories

There are several things that make great content great. It might resonate closely with the audience – especially true of emotive or humorous content. It could be visually stunning, something that stands out against other content, such as a natural wonder, dazzling colours or an optical illusion. It may feature someone your audience likes, someone well known or the company founder. At a more basic level, pictures of people go down very well!

Universal language

The visual nature of Instagram means your content has the potential to reach a global audience, transcending language barriers and cultural differences.

In addition, the public nature of the platform results in more viral content because there's no limit to who can see it and share it. Instagram has one of the highest engagement rates in the social media world, which means your content has the potential to really fly and reach a lot of people.

The majority of users will consume your content one piece at a time, whenever it appears in their feed or as they're browsing stories. The quality of your content and the extent to which it impresses or resonates with an audience member dictates how it is engaged with. In the world of social media, we're always concerned with traction: the interest, engagement and reach a post can attract.

The algorithm

Instagram's algorithm dictates what appears and when on each user's feed, so it's obviously a crucial element of post-planning and creation. The algorithm uses a variety variable to assess the relevance of posts and to work out what it should show to whom.

Initial traction on a post suggests to Instagram that the content is high quality and relevant to certain people. This means it will be shown prominently to more people. If these people engage with the post, the signals are reinforced and the post will go further and further. The algorithms on social networks proliferate the exposure of the best content, and it is through this that we see the phenomenon of viral content.

However, this isn't quite how the algorithm operates; it just appears that way. The algorithm works on an individual basis. It is used to assess which content should make it on to your feed, with reference to the accounts you follow, the accounts you tend to engage with and the kind of content you generally like. It also considers the popularity of content around the platform and the likelihood that you'll like it too.

Essentially, every piece of content that you could be shown is scored against your personal application of the algorithm; the higher the score, the more prominently a piece of content is shown.

What all this means is that your content stands the best chance of being shown on an individual's feed the more popular and relevant to that person Instagram deems it to be. This boils down to creating content that is relevant to your target audience and generates traction.

The people decide

The nature of your following has a huge impact on how effective your content appears to be. Identical posts could be shared from two different accounts and they'd get entirely different responses and results. If the post was shared by an account with 50,000 followers and the subject matter and style is what those followers have come to expect from that account, it will likely perform very well. It will generate hundreds of likes in a matter of minutes, thrusting the post onto the feeds of its followers and beyond. Comments roll in, people get mentioned in the comments, other accounts repost it to their feed, winning new fans and followers.

Another account with just 1,000 followers, who generally expect a different genre of post, see the same image and caption. A slow trickle of likes come in over the course of an hour, but there's nothing telling Instagram that this post deserves distribution far and wide. The account may even lose some followers that find the content irrelevant.

These two very different results have manifested from the same post. Context is everything.

The four steps to creating great content

This chapter is split into the following four areas:

1. Post-planning
2. Creating Great Content
3. Captions and Hashtags
4. Finding New Ideas

Focusing on these elements will make it easier to share great content and take your account's content to the next level.

Post-planning

Having a plan for your content will help with the flow of your output and post consistency, as well as taking advantage of events and seasonality.

Creating Great Content

Great content will enable you to reach new audiences, grow your account and elevate your profile and influence.

Captions and Hashtags

With your visual content now on point, you'll need compelling captions and the right hashtags. Captions provide that all-important context to posts. Hashtags will get your posts seen by more people – and the right people.

Finding New Ideas

Composing a piece of engaging content is far easier when the subject matter is exciting and relevant. Regularly posting high-quality content is challenging because sometimes you simply don't know what to post about. We'll finish this section by helping you find inspiration for fresh new ideas.

Post-planning

When it comes to consistently sharing high-value and effective content, it helps to create a plan of execution. The time at which you post matters. How often you post matters. Which content you post when matters. Getting these things right does not happen by accident.

Posting the perfect schedule of content requires planning, especially if you're going to keep it up over any length of time. You'd be hard-pushed to find a brand with a strong Instagram feed that doesn't have some semblance of plan or content calendar. Note that this doesn't have to remove the spontaneity of the platform, which is certainly one of its allures. Instead, it will become easier to take advantage of opportunities because the day-to-day content is taken care of.

Thinking ahead

If you're investing time and effort in creating strong individual pieces of content, make the most of them by getting them to work together. Having a logical flow of content requires you to plan ahead of time, factoring in key events for your brand as well as key calendar dates.

Seasonality plays a role for most brands and almost all are able to leverage key dates, whether they're national days, public holidays or something sector-specific. Seasonal and topical posts generally go down well on social media and they usually provide ample fodder for content ideas.

Having a macro view of the year that highlights focal points each month or quarter creates some order and provides clarity for you on the micro week-to-week and day-to-day level. What you want is a kind of roadmap; you may take some detours, but ultimately you know where you're going.

Planning your content ahead of time has many benefits.

- ◄ It's more efficient to plan posts in one session.
- ◄ It ensures cohesion in terms of achieving set goals.
- ◄ It helps identify gaps or shortcomings in your content.
- ◄ Having some pre-planned content allows for focus on spontaneous content when needed.
- ◄ It facilitates even spacing of posts and post content.
- ◄ It allows prep time for significant calendar events.

But looking ahead is not the only element of planning. We also need to look at the timing and frequency of posts.

It's all in the timing

Timing is crucial on Instagram. The time at which your account shares a post has a significant bearing on when your audience is likely to see that post. This is because timeliness, or recency, is a key factor in the algorithm. The vast majority of engagements tend to happen in the minutes and hours immediately after posting and the nature and number of these engagements influence the trajectory of that post.

Posting while your audience is fast asleep is a sure way to minimise that initial spike in engagement and reduce the potential reach of the post. On the other hand, posting at peak times may not be optimal either because there's simply so much noise on the platform and competition from other accounts. Finding the most productive time slot is a balancing act, but we don't have to guess.

Adopting a more rigorous posting schedule makes it easier to identify trends in response and performance. It may also indicate changes in your audience's behaviour. For example, if you always post at either 6pm or 8pm, you are holding your post times constant. This enables you to interpret key sensitivities between these two times on a daily basis and over time. A scattergun approach to timing makes this kind of analysis almost impossible.

The eight rules in this section will look at combining all of the elements described above in your post-planning.

1. When to post

Before 2016, Instagram posts were displayed in chronological order, with the most recent at the top. This meant that every post from everyone you followed appeared in your feed, in the order in which they were posted.

Now Instagram uses an algorithm to decide which posts you see and in which order. It will most likely show you updates from your closest friends and best-loved brands as soon as they are posted, but more distant acquaintances or brands you're not completely aligned with might appear less often.

Once you have your post ready – you've selected the filter, written your caption and added your hashtags – the next decision is when to post it. The algorithm now means that if someone doesn't see your post straight away, it might appear on their feed later, the next time they are online. However, those first few likes are a big signal to Instagram of how popular your post is likely to be.

Consider a post that gains 100 likes within the first 30 minutes, compared to one that gains five likes within the first 30 minutes. Because the first 30 minutes are so important, it makes sense to post when it stands the most chance of being seen straight away.

According to Hubspot, the best day to post on Instagram is Thursday, not just at 3pm, but at 5am, 11am, and 4pm. However, this differs between accounts.

For Instagram stories, each one stays on your profile for 24 hours so it will hit all time zones. However, high engagement early on will signal popularity to Instagram, so the same rules still apply.

CONSIDERATIONS TO MAKE WHEN DECIDING WHEN TO POST

1. **The schedule of your followers.** Who are your followers and when are they active online? Parents, students and young professionals, for example, will each have different daily routines and be online at different times throughout the day, depending on their other commitments.

2. **Time zones.** If your account serves followers in different countries spanning multiple time zones, you can be strategic about when you post to best reach them. For an account with followers in the USA and UK, for example, the UK afternoon might be optimal because it's also during waking hours in the USA.

3. **Your own availability.** As your account grows, you will need to respond to comments, and posting just before you go to bed will mean you can't reach them for eight hours. Consider choosing posting times when you have space for community management afterwards.

4. **Past performance.** When you post, monitor how well that post does in the first 30 minutes and beyond. Look through your feed and cross-reference the day and time you posted with how popular that post was. Over time you should see patterns, which you can use to dictate your posting schedule going forward.

NOTE: don't use any of the above as an excuse not to post. If it's great content, it will gain attention. Instagram will be aware that it's great content and show it to more people. Altering the posting time contributes to its success, but the quality of the post still remains the main factor.

2. How often to post

Choose the posting frequency that fits your individual schedule and availability, and space your posts evenly throughout the week.

For a brand account, it's preferable that you post to your feed every day, but not at the expense of quality. For an account depicting you personally, post to your feed four to six times per week, with Instagram stories on top of this. This means your followers regularly see your posts and are reminded of your existence, but also that you have a life outside of Instagram.

STRATEGIES FOR POSTING FREQUENCY

- ✈ Start by posting less often, then build up gradually as you build your Instagram prowess.

- ✈ Initially, aim to post every four days, then every three, then two, then every day. Set goals for when you'd like to reach each stage and plan accordingly.

- ✈ Put your posting days in your diary so you don't miss them.

See Instagram activity as a marathon rather than a sprint, and think long term. The goal is a sustainable schedule that is easily achieved without it feeling like a chore. It's better to space out fewer posts over a longer period of time than post one per day for three days then nothing for two weeks.

Going over 30 days without posting means you have an 'inactive account'. If any of your followers are using automated or bot tools, this is when they'll start to unfollow automatically.

3. Getting help from others

The term 'Instagram husband' is used to describe the long-suffering person behind the camera. Behind every great Instagram feed there is someone who has taken multiple photos to get that perfect post.

An Instagram teammate sees the perfect opportunity and takes the shot, offers great ideas, or always interacts. They will bolster your efforts and add additional thought and energy to your feed.

FINDING THE PERFECT INSTAGRAM TEAMMATES

- Tell a trusted friend that you're trying to build up your Instagram. If you're the subject of your feed, ask for their help in taking candid images.
- Locate your photographer friends or colleagues. Enlist their professional help in creating ideas for images. Ask them about images that they'd love to emulate.
- Agree reciprocal likes or comments. Make an Instagram pact whereby you each commit to being the first like or comment on each other's Instagram updates, to ensure they always have a base level of engagement.
- Educate your Instagram teammates as to what you're looking for in a picture. Tell them why you do and don't like a certain shot.

If you need to ask a stranger to take a picture for you, say at a tourist attraction or restaurant, follow these guidelines:

- Look for someone who already has a good camera. The chances are, they'll know how to work yours and they'll understand framing and composition.
- Set everything up for them. Configure your settings or mode so they just need to point and shoot.
- Give direction. Tell them what you'd like the picture to include and where you'd like them to stand to take it.
- Ask for a countdown. Ask them to take three pictures, and to do a three-second countdown to each one. That way, you are prepared and you have options.

4. Planning your content in advance

It's likely that you know what is coming up for your brand over the next six months. Perhaps you have events booked in, launches scheduled, key meetings or milestones planned.

Your Instagram updates will feel effortless if you can map your posts against your forthcoming schedule. It takes out the biggest obstacle which is not knowing what to post about.

HOW TO GET AHEAD WITH CONTENT PLANNING

- Get your diary out and see what is coming up in the next few months.
- For key events, milestones, dates and meetings, identify an appropriate picture you could take.
- Add the activity of taking the picture to your diary. Then add the activity of posting the picture.
- If you're going on a trip, plan when you will post based on what you're doing.
- Plan celebration posts. For example, if your brand has an anniversary or milestone coming up, is launching a new product or service, hiring a new team member or moving premises.
- If you are the focus of your account, include personal events too.

MARCH

08 Monday

Meeting with Daniel
- Take selfie at lunch

09 Tuesday

10 Wednesday

Georgia's first day
(Take welcome to the team picture)

11 Thursday

Autumn collection photoshoot
Take behind the scenes image of photoshoot

12 Friday

13 Saturday

★ Trip to London - Take landscape
image of London eye plus river

14 Sunday

Over time, you will automatically see opportunities for Instagram pictures in everything you do. It will mean you can plan for the moment, take the shot, then continue with your day safe in the knowledge that you have what you need.

Planning in advance will take the pressure off because you'll be on top of your content schedule. It will mean you spend less time worrying about what to post and how to get the perfect content and more time enjoying your real life.

5. Scope out national and international days

Just as you personally have a calendar of events and milestones coming up, so too does your industry and country. There's also a global calendar of international days, as well as whatever is going on in the news at any given time.

Make the most of these posting opportunities by identifying them in advance, assessing their relevance to your brand, then organising a post to accompany them. Add the day and the image to your calendar.

POSTING OPPORTUNITIES INCLUDE:

International holidays and events
Christmas, New Year, Valentine's Day, Singles Day, Easter, Diwali, bank holidays, back to school. Even the start of sporting events including world cups, Olympics and the Superbowl.

International days of relevance
There's one for almost everything you can think of. The (endless) list includes International Donut Day, Global Entrepreneurship Week and National Sibling Day. And every year there is a Pantone colour of the year, a sports personality of the year and a most-Googled phrase of the year.

Current affairs

At any given time there will be upcoming events, speeches, revelations and occurrences in the news. Although I recommend most accounts avoid divisive or political commentary, look out for opportunities to put your spin on newsworthy events.

Industry-relevant days

Every year, without fail, events will occur in your industry that your audience will expect you to know about. Specific conferences or shows, when certain news is announced, when key people make key decisions, and so on.

An education lawyer might create posts relating to her country's school and education timetable, including posts relevant to examinations, education authority decision timings, and term or holiday dates.

Someone working in the fashion industry might wish to stay abreast of seasons, new trends in colours, fabrics and textures, as well as industry shows and events taking place all over the world.

6. Schedule content to maintain a consistent presence

Your Instagram feed is not your whole life and should not be treated as such. Use your Instagram to share highlights, build your brand and keep in touch, but don't let it replace real-life interactions and activity. Scheduling content can help with this.

WHY SCHEDULE?
Scheduling content allows you to be in control of your Instagram, instead of the other way around. It means you can batch your efforts and organise your posting in an effective and efficient way. It also means you can still be posting when you're asleep, busy or offline. Scheduling helps you plan in advance and keep consistency without interrupting your schedule.

HOW TO SCHEDULE
Use approved third-party tools: create your posts, including filters, captions and hashtags, then choose the time at which they will be sent. Recommended tools include Hopper and Buffer, both of which have been approved by Instagram for this purpose.

Choose your scheduling times based on analysis of when your audience are likely to be online, as well as using data from past performance.

- Keep a folder on your computer or phone with the images you want to post. Once a week, schedule them all in at once, so your week's Instagram content is sorted.
- Alternatively, schedule half of your posts, meaning your basic presence is taken care of while still leaving material for ad hoc posts as you see fit.
- Schedule posts on the same theme in advance, for efficiency. For example, if every Wednesday you share a tip relevant to your work, scheduling will mean you can write ten at once and schedule them for the next ten Wednesdays.

7. Identify content series and themes

Introducing a new concept: the content series, a selection of posts that share a common theme.

The content series is a powerful tool because it helps create consistency in your posting, and signals future posts to your followers, while removing barriers to posting by taking care of much of the thought process. It also positions your account as intentional and serious about success, which can be impressive and aspirational.

Content series could consist of the same type of post or idea on the same day of the week, following some of the popular Instagram hashtags:

- #MotivationMonday or PositivityMonday
- #WorkplaceWednesday
- #ThrowbackThursday
- #SelfieSaturday
- #OutfitOfTheDay

Other ideas for themes might include:

- a tip or guidance post on the same date each month
- a newsworthy item or current affairs commentary post twice a month
- new product launches, team member birthdays or anniversaries
- one or two days per month when you share case studies of work you have carried out, that you are most proud of.

Once you commit to your content series or theme, stick with it and don't miss any out; you don't have to commit forever. Content series can last for a duration of your choosing, so you could opt for one month of one series, then move on to another. If you're super organised, you could plan your whole year's worth of content based on 8–12 content themes. These could be related to the seasons, different aspects of your brand, or just different messaging you want to cover in each month or six-week period.

8. Planning a grid or theme to your feed

Your Instagram grid consists of your Instagram feed posts. Referring to the 'grid' itself means considering how each individual post looks when part of a collection.

Whether displayed on mobile or desktop Instagram, your feed will always consist of rows of three posts across the width of the screen. This means that there is room for being creative with feed patterns.

I recommend making a strict policy for your grid and moving everything else to an Instagram story.

FEED: polished, perfectly taken pictures and videos

STORY: behind the scenes, messy, not edited, more random

Think of your feed as your website and ensure every post and how the grid looks as a whole represents you and your brand and what you stand for. Visit your Instagram account as an onlooker and take a glance: are you happy with the look and feel?

THEMING YOUR FEED

Patterns

Let's say that every other post you publish is an inspirational quote. In your feed, this will give a patterned effect, like a chessboard. You can also post images that span a few different posts, so that one big image is seen when the feed is viewed together.

Colour scheme

Being consistent with the colour palette you use in your individual posts will mean your whole feed fits the same vibe. Perhaps you could move these colours in different directions depending on the seasons.

Specific filters

Using the same filter for each post will give an overall feed consistency, which helps create a consistent brand feel.

Borders

Choosing specific borders for each of your posts will give an arty effect when your feed is viewed in its entirety.

Planning your grid in this way is a commitment that requires all future posts to fit the theme, otherwise it will look messy. Before you commit to a theme, make sure you are aware of what it means for your posting schedule.

Ben & Jerry's, USA & UK
@BENANDJERRYS
@BENANDJERRYSUK

Kathryn Griffin, Assistant digital marketing manager

The global ice cream brand connecting with fans over a scoop, wherever they are.

Ben & Jerry's aim is to make the best possible ice cream in the nicest possible way. Ben & Jerry's UK team joined Instagram in 2015, marking the ice cream activist's second Instagram account, with the debut US account launched in 2011. We delve into their content strategy based on their strong brand and social mission.

TELL ME ABOUT YOUR INSTAGRAM ACCOUNT AND WHAT IT'S DESIGNED TO DO.

We aim to love our fans more than they love us! Instagram is all about connecting with our fans; giving them news of products, talking to them about the issues that are important to us and having fun. Instagram is a great space for us to get to know our fans better and engage more with them.

Ben & Jerry's operates a three-part mission where the product, economic and social parts of the business are equally important, and this shapes our approach to social media. Instagram has developed into a priority channel for us globally and it's where we showcase all things Ben & Jerry's: delicious looking ice cream, recipe ideas, fun content, and values-led education including the social justice causes we champion.

CAN YOU TAKE US THROUGH YOUR PROFILE AND PICTURES?

The profile is intentionally simple, designed to be easy to find and instantly recognisable as authentic. We have the same profile picture across all our countries' Instagram accounts for consistency. We post regularly, at least 4-5 times per week across stories and feed per account, sometimes more if we have events or news we can't wait to tell our fans about. We split our updates into four main content buckets; flavours, social mission, heritage & foundation and fun!

We focus mainly on photography on Instagram as that is how our fans are using the channel too, but we blend in illustrations where relevant, for example in a stories quiz or for talking about issues rather than ice cream. We incorporate video and animation, knowing that even a small bit of movement can be both fun and thumb-stopping to capture followers' attention. We like to approach social copy and photography in the style of a passionate amateur – we don't want to be overly polished; we want to reflect how our fans are posting and using the platform. We analyse our creative and our copy before posting and occasionally we can predict how a post will perform - new flavours are always winners. However, because we like to try new things, our followers often surprise us and we can get it wrong sometimes.

Our use of Instagram means we deliver our three-part mission in increasingly fun and interesting ways and we will always embrace experimentation. We are inspired by our heritage and our founders and we love to learn from other values-led businesses and occasionally other foodie companies too. We won't stop innovating because that is who we are. We won't stop talking about the issues we are passionate about regardless of post-performance.

HOW HAS YOUR ACCOUNT EVOLVED SINCE ITS CREATION?

Stories have increasingly become a bigger part of what we do and we are creating more stories than ever. Having multiple frames and being able to capture our followers' attention for longer in full screen format allows us to go into more depth, especially on more complex social justice topics. The swipe up function to link directly to our website for more information means their experience with us can continue.

We are increasingly using stories for recipe videos, and adding features such as GIFs, polls and quizzes always encourage nice engagement from our fans. Stories only being live for 24 hours allows us to experiment without risk and is a great way to bring our followers into any events we might attend and make them feel like they are there too. We use stories to repost content that our followers tag us in. It's a nice way to make them feel a part of the Ben & Jerry's community and we love what they come up with.

HOW DO YOU ENGAGE WITH YOUR COMMUNITY AND DOES THIS LINK TO SALES?

We keep an eye on our comments and reply where we think it will provide value to our fans or make them laugh. We have fun with them! We have seen the whole business grow as our online community has grown and believe that staying true to what Ben & Jerry's stands for is a big part of that. We represent the human voice of the brand through all our social accounts – Instagram specifically was made for connecting with friends and family so we want our fans to feel like we are part of their world rather than an interruption.

We want to connect and engage with our audience but don't necessarily need something in return. It isn't all about the sales. Plus, tracking sales is difficult as we don't own our own retail stores. Instagram is often part of paid social campaigns; our US account ran one of Instagram's first ever ad campaigns, but we don't tend to boost content from our organic channel as this arena is all about connecting with our fans outside the paid space. Our paid media has specific KPIs and audiences and whilst we are sure there is overlap, we approach these two spaces differently and use them for different reasons.

We see spikes in the growth of our Instagram account with the launch of new flavours; our followers often tag their friends in posts and we see some increase from there, but we generally see steady growth through posting regularly and providing a variety of engaging content.

WE INCORPORATE
VIDEO AND ANIMATION,
KNOWING THAT EVEN A
SMALL BIT OF MOVEMENT
CAN BE BOTH FUN AND
THUMB-STOPPING TO
CAPTURE FOLLOWERS'
ATTENTION.

WE ANALYSE OUR
CREATIVE AND OUR
COPY BEFORE POSTING
AND OCCASIONALLY
WE CAN PREDICT HOW
A POST WILL PERFORM
– NEW FLAVOURS ARE
ALWAYS WINNERS.

Creating Great Content

First and foremost, Instagram is a content platform. Much of your success will be determined by how well your content is received by your audience and how much further its influence reaches. It is in your power to produce content to be proud of, which allows your account to evolve and works to achieve your goals.

Having a huge content budget certainly gives marketers an advantage when it comes to social media management, but for Instagram, you can get 90 per cent of the way there with little or no cost for a number of reasons.

- The majority of your content will be seen on small mobile devices.
- Most images and videos on Instagram are taken on a phone.
- Videos and stories are short.
- Concepts need to be simple to be easily understood while scrolling.
- Catching the eye is achieved in many simple ways.

A cool concept with the right execution, carried out within your means as a brand, is more than sufficient to produce strong content. A lack of studio or film crew is not going to stop you from fulfilling your goals; that's just the icing on the cake.

This section focuses on specific areas of content creation that are accessible to anyone, but may be enhanced with access to a camera or professional photographer. We're going to look at ways to instantly take your content game up a notch, alongside others that will require some time to perfect.

What makes great content?

Defining great content is hard. Beauty is in the eye of the beholder, after all. Great content may help portray your brand as an expert in its field or compel users to make a purchase. Maybe it grows your following by fifty accounts. There are many paths to greatness.

Your first objective is to create a visual that will stop users scrolling their feeds and pay attention. Second is to compel those users to take action – to like, comment or even share.

Even with best practice, not every technique will work for every brand and audience. There will always be an element of testing, retesting, trying new things and perfecting your approach. How your audience responds and how your account grows will be the real indicator of success.

However, almost universally relevant are certain key elements we can look to perfect:

- improving photo quality
- using interesting subject matter, angles and styles
- leveraging a range of photo on Instagram-specific apps
- combining images, collections, videos and stories
- employing popular content tactics.

Quality (nearly) always counts

No Instagram account is totally immune to the need for quality. It is true that superbrands and celebrities can post virtually anything and attract huge post engagement. This is because it adds value to their fans' days simply because it comes from their account. If this is you, then fantastic. For the rest of us, content that wows, entertains, relates and resonates with our target audience will go further.

However your account achieves it, you need to generate buy-in from your audience, combining your strong brand identity with well-put-together content.

This section looks at the visual element of posts and outlines the top ten rules for creating great content.

1. Taking photos

There's no hiding from it. The better the quality of your pictures, the better they will perform on Instagram.

PLANNING
If there are people involved in your shots, have a plan for their wardrobe, facial expressions, hand gestures, posing positions, props and where in the picture they will feature.

If you are shooting products, have a plan for the lighting, the background, the accompanying items, how they are positioned and the impression each shot evokes.

SETTING UP
While a professional camera is always the first choice, the latest smartphones are perfect for taking Instagram pictures.

Use a photo app rather than the Instagram app itself and take practice shots first. Ensure the subject is in focus. Think about composition. Move around to test positioning, control the angle and place the subject prominently in the frame. Use the gridlines to follow the rule of thirds and consider symmetry and framing using surrounding objects.

Think about depth and background. How does the shot compliment or contextualise the main subject? Think about colours: monochromatic, contrasting colours, complementary colours or your specific colour palette.

MODES AND ANGLES
Help your images to stand out best by shooting things in an unusual way. Zoom in on an everyday object so that you see the textures; look at a place or product from a different angle or take a bird's eye view of a lifestyle scene. You can use lines to lead someone's eye within the shot to the main focal point.

Most phone camera have various settings, including portrait mode and zoom, as well as tricks for controlling the focus and lighting before taking each shot. Test each mode, reassess, and only share the pictures that work really well.

LIGHTING
Generally, bright and sharp images are best. Natural lighting is always preferable to flash, but bright sunlight isn't ideal. Early mornings, sunsets and clouds are all great sources of lighting.

To underexpose your photo on an iPhone, tap and hold the brightest area of your phone, which locks in the focus and exposure. It's easier to brighten a dark shot in post-production than it is to darken one that has been overexposed. Include light sources in your planning and look into acquiring suitable hardware to leave less to chance.

POST-PRODUCTION
The better the raw image, the less need there is for filters or other edits. Avoid overediting the image; the goal is to make it look effortless, not overly set up, rehearsed or modified.

Perform basic edits to ensure your pictures are fit for Instagram. Crop, straighten, edit the lighting, colour or shadows and apply the filter or set of rules that you use throughout your feed.

TO FILTER OR NOT TO FILTER?
Using the same filter or set of filters for each image you post means that someone scrolling quickly past content will instantly recognise your brand. This kind of familiarity is priceless. Some of my favourite Instagram accounts use the same filter each time and it looks impressive.

PRACTICE
Practise thinking of the ideas and using each camera function. Look out for special moments, candid action shots, or any other opportunity to take a picture. It might feel hard work at first, but over time it will become a habit.

Practise taking more photos. Try new angles, expressions and lighting and mix up everything outlined so far to test, refine, repeat and create images you're proud of. Sign up to a course or watch some YouTube videos.

2. Supercharge your content with apps

There are hundreds of apps designed for the sole purpose of maximising the effectiveness of your Instagram photos. These apps will help emphasise the hard work you have already put in taking a great image, or replace some of the post-production legwork. They also serve to give variety to your feed.

Boomerang takes a short burst of photos and stitches them together in a mini video that plays forwards and backwards. It is good for capturing short action shots, such as cutting into food. For professional-looking Boomerangs, keep every aspect of your shot still except one. You can also use Boomerang's hidden settings menu to change the resolution and the mode.

Layout is a collage app designed to display multiple images within one image. Open the app, select the images to include and then drag borders and rearrange for maximum effect. Use for creating mood boards, showing multiple angles of products, event images, or the same view at different times of the day.

Snapseed is a photo editing app with an abundance of features and pre-set modes to test out. It professionally edits your images without the need to spend hours on Photoshop.

Instories collates photos, videos, images and words to create downloadable Instagram stories. Use for slideshows, competitions, announcements and launches, or to share messages in a more professional way than Instagram's own text settings.

Repost lets you share someone else's image to your feed while captioning and crediting them perfectly. Find an Instagram post you want to share to your own feed, copy the link and paste it into Repost. Repost then adds an attribution mark and copies the caption, ready for you to post effortlessly. Use for sharing customer pictures, inspiration posts or building your community by promoting and sharing the work of others.

Over can be used to add frames, borders and text overlays to your images. Edit the text and the colours to perfectly match your brand. Use for sharing quotes, key information, testimonials, product specifics or updates.

3. Hardware

Camera phone technology has developed rapidly in recent years, much of it driven by the need to take awesome photos for social media. The quality of the device you use to take photos undoubtedly makes a difference to the quality of the images you can capture, but there are other items of hardware that supercharge the quality further.

Investing in your own photo-taking space or gaining access to a studio will almost certainly give you better results. They'll also have a range of lighting set-ups and accessories for you to experiment with.

HARDWARE INVESTMENTS
A good camera or camera phone will improve your content almost immediately.

Lens attachments allow you to create a range of images and it's possible to buy them as smartphone attachments. Try a fisheye lens and a zoom lens and also look for those that minimise glare and reflections.

Lighting is everything. Look for vanity or beauty lights, reflectors and diffusers to help you soften the light you're working with.

For setting up images to be proud of, use a **tripod** to fix your camera and a **bluetooth clicker** to capture images even if you're not behind it.

If budget and appetite allows, invest in a **slider rail** for short product videos with high production value, or a **drone** for overhead shots and perfect action videos.

4. Attention to detail

A keen eye for detail will elevate the quality of your imagery. Spotting blemishes, creases or stains on outfits or random objects in the background of your set-up will pay dividends. Not only will it prevent a detail ruining an otherwise perfectly good image, but it will save time trying to remove it in post-production.

With every shot you take, check what is in the background. Avoid taking selfies with a messy bed, or even a toilet in shot. Office backgrounds featuring untidy desks or sensitive information on the walls are a no-no. Check to see if there are any other brands visible, or anything else that could distract.

Negative space, otherwise known as a plain background, is generally better for likes and engagement. However, avoid pure white because this makes your images look like catalogue shots, which screams promotion.

For many shots, using portrait mode on your camera phone is a good option because it automatically blurs the background and focuses the attention purely on the subject in focus.

TOP TIPS
- ◀ Put the most important aspect of your shot in the centre.
- ◀ Use portrait mode to blur the background around the focal point.
- ◀ Create flat-lay images for a birds-eye view of products or scenes.
- ◀ Remove labels or text on accessories to avoid distraction.
- ◀ Ask a friend about the first thing they notice when they look at a specific image.
- ◀ Feature props prominently or adjust lighting so they appear brighter.
- ◀ Tidy up first. Put miscellaneous items away and clean all surfaces.
- ◀ Wait until people or clouds have moved out of the way.

5. Hire a photographer

Employing a professional photographer will give you a bank of high-quality images to use across social media for the next month or even year.

FINDING A SUITABLE PHOTOGRAPHER

- ◂ Check out Airbnb experiences. Look at photography experiences in your home town or somewhere you are visiting and send the photographer a message.
- ◂ Ask your photographer friends if they'd like to do a shoot.
- ◂ Find photographers on Instagram whose pictures you like and approach them about a shoot.
- ◂ Look at the accounts whose content you love and see if they have tagged their photographer in their images.

CHECKLIST PRIOR TO SHOOTING

- ◂ Write a brief of the shots you want to get and send it to the photographer in good time, to allow them to prepare.
- ◂ Include specifics such as desired image dimensions, the purpose of the shoot and other images for inspiration.
- ◂ If you are the subject of the images, take a change of clothes. Mixing up your wardrobe will make it seem as though the shots are from different shoots. Do the same with make-up, hair and accessories.
- ◂ Ask the photographer about their equipment, so you know if they have specialist pieces you can utilise.
- ◂ Take all the props you will need: products, product accessories, anything that will be included in the shots to make them look as natural as possible.
- ◂ Look at the photographer's previous work for inspiration, including images or photo effects you might want to recreate. Don't be afraid to ask questions and probe into their work and experience.

The key to a successful shoot and having images you're proud of is people, products and places. Have a clear plan for each and make sure everyone is on board with your vision.

6. Make use of popular content ideas

Producing content to fit popular Instagram themes may give you more ideas about what to post, as well as helping each post go further. Some of the most popular themes relate simply to days of the week:

- #ThrowbackThursday
- #AboutLastNight
- #MondayMotivation
- #PhotoOfTheDay
- #QuoteOfTheDay
- #OutfitOfTheDay
- #MindfulMonday
- #TransformationTuesday
- #WisdomWednesday
- #ThankfulThursday
- #SaturdayShoutOut

These types of content series and trends are popular for a reason. In general, brands and users get on board and interact with them. They represent a way of sharing a topic or theme that is familiar and appealing to audience members.

Experiment with tried-and-tested hashtags to explore how your brand can leverage them. You may also be able to find some industry-specific hashtags and topics and may even progress to inventing some of your own, which other accounts start to use.

With these ideas, you're not sacrificing any originality. The key is to be original within the context of the theme. Fresh ideas and unique takes on the trend are very cool.

Look for excuses to post rather than excuses not to post. Every hashtag you can make use of is another reason to send out a great post that engages your audience, attracts new people to your account and reminds your followers who you are and what you stand for.

7. Posts with multiple pictures

Collections of images are an interesting alternative to single-image posts. You can post up to ten images at the same time and they'll show up as a gallery-like collection. These may be employed in several scenarios:

- Multiple product shots, showcasing different angles, variations or uses of the same product, or comparing different products.
- Similar images of a scene or subject, either from different angles, times of the day or year, before or after pictures, or images that show progress in some way.
- Event pictures, with images of the location, setting, people, entertainment or speakers.
- Changing one thing within the image each time, such as the same product being used in different ways, or the same person with different backgrounds.
- To demonstrate progress. The same metric or aspect of your business over time; perhaps a team shot each year, or images of something being built or the development of an idea.
- Delivering longer pieces of information, or a story. For example, the blurb of a new book with a different image for each sentence, a strategy or plan of action, or a novel way to explain more technical aspects of a product.
- When some of the images won't work on their own. If you know that certain pictures perform best on your feed, but want to add variety without compromising engagement.

These posts are interactive, and individuals who stop to peruse the gallery are spending much longer on these updates than others.

Make sure you use your best image first, but bear in mind that Instagram will show the next one to a user who scrolled past the post first time round. This means you have a slightly better chance of engagement. If the images are sequential in some way, they may not always be shown in that order.

8. Using videos

Video content is popular on social media. Within 24 minutes of the Instagram video post feature being launched in 2013, five million videos were posted. Sponsored Instagram videos generate, on average, three times more comments than sponsored images.

For your own brand, video content on Instagram must be well executed to be effective. There are three options:

- Feed videos, up to 1 minute long
- Story videos, up to 15 seconds long
- Instagram TV (IGTV), up to 60 minutes long

Ensuring the quality of videos is trickier than for still images and there are also fewer options available in terms of editing. In any case, avoid hand-held phone footage, other than for the most candid of Instagram stories.

TOP TIPS

- **Sound:** most Instagram users watch videos on mute, so ensure they make sense without sound, or look compelling enough to get viewers to grab headphones. You can add the instruction 'Sound on' to Instagram stories, but there's no guarantee people will comply.
- **Text:** add text to your video, just as you would a photo, to explain what's going on. Include bullet point overlays of the key messages or add subtitles to the dialogue.
- **Signposting:** use the caption to direct viewers to look out for specific occurrences at specific timestamps.
- **Speed:** use slow-motion, fast-forward or stop-motion effects to get the message across in a novel way. Stop-motion in particular plays to short attention spans because a lot can happen in a short space of time.
- **Media training:** if you feature in your Instagram videos, practise talking directly to the camera in a confident way so that you engage with viewers. Smile and relax as you deliver your message, and get a second opinion or invite constructive criticism from a trusted friend or colleague.

9. Tips to ramp up your engagement

There are certain trends to consider when it comes to improving the engagement received on posts and a range of tactics you can implement to boost your account's chances of appearing prominently on any individual's feed.

Pictures featuring faces receive, on average, 38 per cent more likes than those without. If the account is for a personal brand, or for a brand associated with a prominent individual, images of the relevant person will perform significantly better than those without. The account's audience has a connection with that individual and the personal nature of the post will boost performance.

Statistically, there is a trend towards images that are cooler in tone and those that have a bluish hue as opposed to reddy-orange. Brighter and lighter images tend to perform better, on average, than darker images, but there's mixed evidence about the effect of colour saturation. These elements can be edited in post-production as well as captured in the original take.

There's also evidence to support the use of highly textured images, where it's possible to see the texture of objects as opposed to when the subjects are smooth. Having a clearer background or more white space also appears to help engagement, as does a post incorporating a single dominant colour as opposed to multiple colours.

10. Share positively

Be positive. Always. Be a force for good. Radiate positivity. Talk positively about people, places and products. Talk positively about other brands or collaborations or the work that you are doing. Imagine how you want someone to feel when they consume your content, and make sure you back that up, always.

Complaints in comments, negative posts or backhanded and passive-aggressive captioning just isn't cool and won't serve to uplift you or others. It won't create a brand that people want to follow or talk about and it will earn your account a reputation you don't want.

Add value and post to serve. Aim to be the boost someone needs; the account they look forward to hearing from. Channel positivity through everything you post and look on the bright side.

POSITIVITY RULES
- Your vibe attracts your tribe, so make it good.
- Negativity is a reflection on you as a person or brand.
- Use your Instagram to radiate positivity and good vibes.
- Your audience might not remember what you posted, but they will remember how your account made them feel.

A recent trend has been to leverage vulnerability and tell stories of tough times in order to gain sympathy or to emphasise today's achievements. This is certainly effective in attracting comments, but it's a fine line to tread. Vulnerability can certainly be a positive strength, but you cannot employ this tactic regularly, and it may not be the right kind of message for optimal brand portrayal.

If vulnerability and overcoming adversity are part of your story and you can work out how to use it in the right way for a greater good, then fine. If it's not part of your story, don't fabricate hardships to win sympathy or followers. You be you. The most important message is authenticity.

Captions and Hashtags

Captions

The caption is a fundamental element of the anatomy of an Instagram post, yet it receives a fraction of the attention compared with its visual counterpart, which is by far the most prominent part of the post. The caption is similar to the text in a Facebook post or a tweet; the big difference is that Instagram posts *must* include an image, and this demotes the importance of the text to a degree. Yet it still plays a vital role in content optimisation and strategy execution, helping to convey brand values and voice and encouraging an audience to take a desired action.

All feed posts (images, collections and videos) have space for a caption; only Instagram stories do not, but they have other ways to add commentary. Within captions you can add text, symbols, line spacing, emojis and hashtags, so there is huge scope for creativity. Captions can be used to:

- add contextual information
- add humour
- pose a question
- tell a story
- offer a discount or announce a competition
- provide a call to action
- tag and mention other accounts
- give thanks.

Sometimes it's just not possible to communicate these sentiments through imagery alone.

The caption is where you're able to tie in your brand's tone of voice to help deepen your relationship with your audience and their understanding of your brand. It's also the perfect opportunity to work towards some of your account and commercial goals.

There are many different tactics that can be employed when it comes to writing a caption, from a single emoji to an almost essay-like pitch to win business and attention. Captions are also where you can include your selection of accompanying hashtags, although you could add these as a comment, too. Your challenge is to learn what compels your audience to take the action you would like them to in a way that remains in line with your brand's ethos.

Hashtags

Hashtags serve many important purposes on the platform, but mainly act to categorise content, making it easier to find. Hashtags undoubtedly aid the reach of brand accounts and help acquire new followers in their niche, especially when a piece of content performs well among posts using a specific hashtag.

There is certainly a science to using hashtags, including some rules to follow in order to stand the best chance of getting the most out of them. There are also some pitfalls to avoid. Add hashtags to every feed post you share and include them in stories, too.

Don't underestimate the power of words. In fact, it's possible to focus heavily on captions as the primary way to communicate with your audience. You will have likely seen posts on Instagram in which the image has been more symbolic in nature and where the real emphasis has been on the caption. There's a whopping 2,200 character limit on Instagram captions, which translates to over 400 words and you can use as many as 30 hashtags. Some accounts really make the most of these limits when it suits their needs.

In this section we're going to explore seven ways to make the most of the written word to enhance your awesome visuals and how captions and hashtags can work for your brand.

1. Conduct hashtag research

Don't leave your hashtag game to chance. Research
the perfect combination of hashtags to accompany
your posts ahead of time.

THE MOST IMPORTANT FACTORS OF HASHTAGS
- How often they are used.
- Their relevance to your sector.
- The content shared using them.
- If they work for your brand.
- Any accompanying or complementary hashtags.

Each of these factors requires research, but there are tools
and techniques to make this easier.

RESEARCHING HASHTAGS
- Write down six words and phrases that embody the
  content shared on your account.
- Using a hashtag research tool (see oppsosite), type them
  in, one at a time.
- Make a note of a further six hashtags that relate to
  each of your original six.

HASHTAG TOOLS

RiteTag, Hashtagify, AllHashtag and Sistrix all enable you to type in a hashtag and see ideas of related hashtags, as well as the number of uses for each one.

For example, searching 'travel' brings results for: travelgram, travelphotography, travelling, travels, travelabout. Searching 'entrepreneur' brings results for: startup, business, success, skills, motivation, grind, and so on.

Researching hashtags you've already used is also invaluable in planning your hashtag selection going forward. If your account is a business profile, click to 'view insights' under each post, and scroll down to 'discovery' to see how many impressions come from the hashtags used. Monitor how this changes when you use different combinations of hashtags. Look at both the absolute number and the number as a percentage of total impressions.

TOP TIP Use hashtags relating to the same words in different languages. An Instagram feed focused on nature and flowers might also use the hashtags #blume, #fleurs and #fiore.

2. Use a blend of hashtags

A hashtag described as 'popular' means that a large number of accounts use it in posts or search for it. The more popular a hashtag, the more competitive it is, but the greater the potential value for your content.

An account is permitted to use up to 30 hashtags per post. While there is a common-sense argument for using the full quota, studies show that posts with 8-12 perform best in terms of engagement.*

Searching for a specific phrase in Instagram under 'Tags' will show:

◄ how many posts relate to that hashtag
◄ the top posts for that hashtag
◄ the most recent posts for that hashtag
◄ related hashtags
◄ people you know that follow the hashtag
◄ sometimes, Instagram story posts relating to that hashtag
◄ the option to follow that hashtag.

If one of your posts appears in the search results for 'top posts' for a hashtag, this can give your content a boost. However, the more popular the hashtag, the harder this is to achieve, especially if you don't have a large following.

Use a blend of mainstream, niche and super-niche hashtags on each post to cover all bases. This gives you multiple options along the competition/benefit scale. Use the tools explored in your hashtag research, as well as Instagram itself, to select your combination.

I recommend:
- ◀ 4-6 popular hashtags (100,000+ uses)
- ◀ 2–6 niche hashtags (25,000-100,000 uses)
- ◀ 2–6 super-niche hashtags (1,000-25,000 uses)

The more relevant a hashtag to your account, your niche and the content shared, the more you can tip the potential benefit of using that hashtag in your favour.

HASHTAGS IN STORIES
You can use hashtags in Instagram stories, either by using the hashtag sticker and editing the text, or by typing '#' followed by your term as regular text. It's possible to add up to 10 hashtags to an Instagram story, and you can shrink them down or hide them behind gifs or stickers so they don't clutter your content.

If the story is popular, it has the potential to be included as a story for that hashtag, which can result in further views and engagement.

* However, there may be other factors at play in this research, such as very large accounts gaining high engagement levels anyway.

3. Keep some hashtags consistent, change some up

Use a broader range of hashtags over time to put your account in front of a larger audience and to increase your brand reach and the chance of gaining new followers. Keep in mind the following.

- ◀ It is not optimal to share content with the exact same hashtags every time.
- ◀ Different content commands different use of hashtags.
- ◀ Content should be as relevant to the hashtag combination as possible.

If you have some brand-, product- or industry-specific hashtags that you deem relevant for every post you share, that's fine. Keep some the same but make sure you rotate some fresh ones in as well.

Imagine you're explaining your image to someone who can't actually see it. You want to give them the best possible understanding of the image and its context. Over time, hashtagging will become second nature to your content creation endeavours. Get there faster by following the process below.

1. Start with broader hashtags relating to your content and theme.
2. Then go niche. For example, use city and town place names rather than country names, specific dish names rather than types of cuisine, or specific gym exercises rather than general fitness terms.
3. Go super-niche after that. Think about the context, settings, emotions, people and places and the niche phrases used to summarise them.
4. You can even use ultra-niche specific hashtags for humour, to add further interest, or to kick-start hashtags you have invented which relate specifically to your brand.

For stylistic purposes, you can choose to add hashtags as the first comment on the post instead of in the caption itself, but you can still only include a total of 30.

AVOID BEING REPETITIVE, IRRELEVANT OR SPAMMY

It's against Instagram's community guidelines to post repetitive content (although what constitutes repetitive is subjective) and your content may end up being flagged if users think you're being spammy or irrelevant or using hashtags incorrectly. This will lead to your content being seen by fewer people.

Allowing users to flag others' use of hashtags as 'not relevant' helps Instagram's filter when it comes to working out what to show people.

TOP TIP Save your popular hashtag lists in a Word document or somewhere on your computer or phone, for ease of copying and pasting at a future date. Check they have formatted correctly and double-check for absolute relevancy to each post.

4. Use longer captions

Strong imagery is what causes an Instagram scroller to stop and take note. However, captions can be the main engagement driver.

Longer captions can serve to capture attention. They enable you to tell more of a story, to contextualise the image or provide further information. Using longer captions, which are widely read by audience members, dramatically increases the time they spend thinking about your brand. This makes understanding, engagement and responses far more likely.

A long and descriptive caption can humanise the post, give it more context and explain why it's there. It doesn't need to be a soul-baring confession; you can simply emphasise why this image, moment or announcement is so important to you and why someone should take note. If posting a long caption is a novelty for your account, this, in itself, may grab their attention.

IDEAS FOR LONG CAPTIONS
- Tell a story about the image and its significance.
- Share lyrics or quotes that summarise the image.
- Share the backstory that led up to this image being taken.
- Inspire, motivate or empower others.
- Give instructions or guidance, broken down by bullet points or numbers.
- Ask for specific feedback or customer insights.
- Present thoughtful or playful questions.

Proofing your captions for errors is especially important for longer prose. Ensure it reads correctly and that it can't be misinterpreted in any way; tone is only ever inferred in text on a screen. Try reading the post as if you were really angry and see if it still works.

Gently break a reader by sectioning the longer caption with new lines, bullet points or emojis, or start with an attention-grabbing question or statement.

FORMATTING CAPTIONS

There are options for how your captions, including hashtags, are formatted on each Instagram post. This flexibility helps you prioritise certain points and have more control over how someone reads the information. Use emojis, space out text, split up paragraphs or use bullet points to style your captions.

TOP TIPS

- ◢ Start your caption with a call to action.
- ◢ Use emojis as bullet points.
- ◢ Put your hashtags at the end.
- ◢ Use manageable paragraphs.
- ◢ Put the most important messages first.
- ◢ Encourage tagging or commenting.
- ◢ Use a series of underscores to add line breaks.
- ◢ Use full stops on new lines to space out paragraphs.

Having a sentence followed by several line spaces before additional information or the hashtags is a popular choice of format because it combines both context and a punchy element.

Instagram also enables you to use different fonts in captions by copying and pasting text from various apps. This can draw attention to your post by giving users something they don't often see. It's also another way to add brand personality.

READ MORE...

Be mindful of the 'read more' function on Instagram. You can only guarantee that someone will see the copy before this. There are approximately three lines of text before the clickable 'read more' button. Prior to this you must either make the key point or engage someone enough to make them want to read on.

5. Punchy caption ideas

When planning your Instagram content and choosing the perfect caption, incorporate some of the following ideas and monitor the responses. For each one, think about your brand and how your audience is likely to interpret the message before posting. Use each one a few times in order to gauge accurately the reaction.

- motivational quotes
- customer testimonials
- thought-leadership quotes or insights
- jokes or puns
- bullet points to explain a concept or process
- stories to take someone on a journey
- a haiku or short poem
- a question, rhetorical or otherwise
- an emoji story
- transcriptions of conversations or interactions
- busting popular myths
- providing facts.

If the purpose of the post is the caption, choose an aesthetically-pleasing and on-brand image that requires little or no explanation. Let the caption do the talking.

Always be authentic, genuine and positive. Avoid being overly cheesy or using ambiguous language or symbols. The caption should make perfect sense to your audience.

TOP TIP If the goal is to evoke a response with your captions, seed the first few. Share your post with your close friends in a private message and ask them to comment on the real thing. Triggering those initial engagements will help set the tone for others to follow.

6. Topical and trending issues and hashtags

Trending hashtags represent an opportunity for brands to be responsive and topical. Making the most of topical and trending hashtags can serve to unite, create common ground and build a community.

Look for stories and breakthroughs relevant to your brand or sector, then think about:

- ◄ your opinion or view on the topic
- ◄ how you can engage in the conversation
- ◄ whether the topic or theme fits with your brand.

Relevant, timely and intelligent content will be rewarded by Instagram's algorithm and putting posts together on short notice can win you a headstart in the trend game. For example, posting about:

- ◄ live events at which winners are announced
- ◄ big events with a large following
- ◄ groundbreaking news or advancements.

Research why a particular hashtag is trending and the kind of posts people are sharing with it. It's really easy to misconstrue a word or phrase and post something on a sensitive matter, which will inevitably be received badly.

TOP TIPS

- ◄ Set up Google Alerts so you receive notifications via email for topics and phrases relevant to your brand.
- ◄ Research Twitter's 'trending' feature. Filter by location to make content super-specific to your target audience.
- ◄ Prepare posts in advance to cover every eventuality of an upcoming revelation, then share the appropriate version.
- ◄ Beware of involving your brand in a trend that just doesn't suit it. Sharing partially relevant content risks looking contrived. If in doubt, sit it out and plan for the next one.

7. Tagging locations, people and brands

Hashtags aren't the only tags worth having a plan for. For each Instagram post or story you share, you have the option to tag locations, people and brands. Each tag adds context and value and can encourage engagement or begin discussions.

LOCATIONS
Location tagging adds information to a post and presents further opportunities to have your content found. Locations display prominently on Instagram posts and stories, adding context as well as potential talking points for comments.

Location tagging means that people searching for that location can see your image in the list of all those taken there. Just like hashtags, Instagram shows the top nine posts for a specific location, so it's an additional opportunity for more post engagement. Making your way into the top nine depends on the competitiveness of the location and your account's dominance, but it offers another channel through which to increase your engagement. Tagging a location in a story may also mean that your story appears on the story of the location itself.

PEOPLE
Behind every great brand is great people. Incorporating those people as part of your content helps them feel proud of their association and can help you reach new audiences. Many clothing brands will tag models, photographers, stylists and make-up artists in images from photoshoots, giving the opportunity to share the story behind the photo and cross-promote to reach new networks.

Tagging existing customers, team members or partners in your images and stories makes them part of your message and presents a confident and united front. Your image will then display on their profile under 'tagged pictures', and they will have the option to reshare your story.

BRANDS

Tagging other brands in your images aligns your brand with theirs and can lead to new relationships. Mentioning the work of complementary brands or those you admire or aspire towards helps put you on their radar and better explain your values and ethos.

Ensure the message and your relationship with the brand you tag is clear. Whether you're a fan or an admirer of their message, or you have a formal partnership, make sure your followers can glean that from your post and how you explain the connection.

For example, an athlete might tag the following in a training video:

- ◀ the gym or venue
- ◀ workout buddies
- ◀ clothing and kit brands or sponsors.

For each post you create, identify the locations, people and brands involved and tag them in, if appropriate.

Can Ahtam, USA
@CANAHTAM

Photographer, born and raised in Istanbul, now living in Los Angeles, USA

The photographer showcasing his work to secure daily enquiries from Instagram.

Can started his account in 2012 to expand his network and exchange inspiration with other creatives around his local neighbourhood in Boston, Massachusetts.

Initially, he only shared photos of stray cats and food from his smartphone. Now based in Los Angeles, Can's images, shot on his Canon Rebel T1i, win thousands of likes and comments as well as regular bookings for his photography services. Here's an insight into how Can grew his account to over 192,000 followers.

WHAT IS THE MAIN PURPOSE OF YOUR ACCOUNT?

My Instagram is a strict photography account, comprised of the photos I take on a daily basis. Whether the photos are from my daily routine or from my travels, I try to share my unique perspective of the world. I never felt comfortable, or found my life interesting enough, to form a lifestyle account about myself.

The theme of my account is simplicity. From the colours to the focal lengths, I want my audience to see the simple yet elegant world we live in and appreciate what it can offer. I make sure my profile reflects this. Life shouldn't be complicated.

HOW HAVE SALES GROWN AS YOUR COMMUNITY HAS GROWN?

With the local community growing on my profile, my numbers for photoshoot bookings have increased. I am contacted daily by brands and individuals for photoshoot bookings.

Part of the increase is due to the demand within Los Angeles, where there are plenty of people in need of content, headshots and editorial shoots.

ARE YOU ABLE TO TRACK SALES FROM INSTAGRAM TO YOUR STORE?

I don't push heavily for sales because that doesn't attract users. I have been selling pre-sets, prints and photoshoots via Instagram, but the photoshoots receive the most enquiries.

My website was created in Squarespace and it allows me to track visitors. About 70 per cent come from Instagram.

WHAT DO YOU DO ON INSTAGRAM EACH WEEK?

My goal used to be three posts a day, which took a long time to manage. However, when I moved to Los Angeles, I decided to focus on my work first and then post and socialise on Instagram as a second priority.

I now post several times a week, which still builds that strong community. I prepare my content the day before and save it as a draft on Instagram. I post around 9am PST because I have community members around the globe. As comments are posted I keep replying and chatting with the folks who comment. This goes on throughout the day until the afternoon.

CAN YOU PREDICT HOW WELL A POST WILL DO BEFORE YOU POST IT?

I get stoked about sharing certain photos because I know that they are not moments that anyone can capture. For example, when I was on top of Haleakala in Hawaii, I had the pleasure of witnessing and capturing a sunrise over the clouds and that made my day. That's very different to shooting a photo of Acorn Street in Boston, which is one of the most photographed streets in the USA.

If the photo has a uniqueness to it, as well as a caption that carries a conversation, I have a good feeling that it will perform well.

DO YOU USE INSTAGRAM ADS TO PROMOTE YOUR CONTENT?

I feel like the algorithm is a mix of technical knowledge and urban myth. My main knowledge on the algorithm is that it is heavily based on interest, relationship and time. With the chronological feed gone, it is definitely tough to make yourself as widely visible. Because of this, I promote content to a targeted audience in my local neighbourhood, primarily for photoshoot bookings and print sales.

HOW DO YOU USE HASHTAGS?

I include three tiers of hashtags in my posts. First there are hashtags that I always keep relevant to the posts I share. For example, for photos of Hawaii I use a related list of place-based hashtags.

Then there are community- and account-related hashtags, including #passionpassport and #beautifuldestinations. Finally, there are photography-related hashtags that I research on a monthly basis, to ensure I always use the latest and most popular ones.

IF THE PHOTO HAS A
UNIQUENESS TO IT, AS
WELL AS A CAPTION
THAT CARRIES A
CONVERSATION, I HAVE
A GOOD FEELING THAT IT
WILL PERFORM WELL.

Finding New Ideas

You've got a plan, you know how to create awesome content, and you can pair it with captivating captions and honed hashtags – but what are you actually going to post about? Naturally, you need to post content that your audience will engage with, but it must also represent your brand and work towards your account's goals. Everything should be on brand and on topic.

All these factors might narrow down the content you share.

For some brands, finding content is easy; there's just Instagrammable stuff happening all the time. However, even those content-rich businesses face challenges. Keeping quality high is one. Ensuring everything fits with the plan and strategy is another. They can also become lazy in what they post because they don't need to think too hard.

The truth is that every brand could benefit from fresh content ideas on Instagram, whether it's a completely new subject or theme, or alternative ways to freshen existing content.

Avoiding poster's block

All things being equal, accounts that only post once or twice a week do not grow as fast as those posting every day. Sometimes finding ideas for potent or articulate content is what's stopping a brand posting more frequently and reaching its full potential. Avoid being in this situation by ensuring you have a constant stream of content and caption ideas, images and videos.

It's also very easy to get stuck in a rut and find yourself posting variations on the same or very similar themes. There's nothing necessarily wrong with that and if that content works, then perfect. However, you might just find that there are other types of content that will work for you, and the variety will improve your overall presence.

Finding inspiration

This section requires you to be open-minded about adopting new content ideas for your brand. We will look at how to use external influences to come up with concepts that might work, to avoid being too insular in your thinking. It may be that a certain element of another brand's content or an image you see could be modified in such a way that it works for your brand.

It's important to find inspiration from a range of sources, combine this with your own concepts, and add your brand's unique touch. You never want to be outright copying what another brand is doing, especially if it's a competitor. Look for that initial spark, then see where you can take it.

Implementing new ideas

Trying out new concepts on your account is exciting, but it also represents a daunting unknown. There are two things to consider.

1. You'll be applying everything we've learned about content creation to these new ideas in order to maximise their effectiveness.

2. You can begin by making tweaks to your style as opposed to completely overhauling your approach.

Given the speed of Instagram, you'll receive feedback on your new content incredibly quickly by way of post engagements. Positive, negative or just different, you can use this information to inform your content decisions moving forward. Sharing more experimental content at times of the day where you know the response rate is fairly reliable enables you to most objectively assess its performance against your usual material.

Here are seven rules to get started.

1. Finding Instagrammable images

Most Instagram posts include places, people or products, or a combination of all three.

PLACES
The world is a beautiful place, with countless opportunities for amazing images – and amazing images are the goal for your Instagram feed. If you know how to look for inspiration, it's easy to find it in the unlikeliest of places.

To find Instagrammable places for your images, try the following:

1. **Google.** Run a search of 'Instagrammable places in [city]' or 'Best pictures at [place]'. Chances are there will be articles containing ideas for you. Take a look through the list and if any fit your brand and palette and would look great on your feed, plan a visit.

2. **Research.** When planning your content in advance, research the places you're going to. That university with the unique buildings or flowers; that meeting with the incredible view. Look it up ahead of time so that you can incorporate it into your plans.

3. **Capitalise on the efforts of others.** Hospitality brands, for example, go to great lengths to make their venues Instagrammable. If it fits with your feed, use it, or you could take inspiration from the settings they have created.

PEOPLE
Think about the people who comprise your brand: clients, customers, teammates, suppliers. Look for opportunities to take interesting photos and tell their stories as part of yours.

PRODUCTS
The worst-performing product shots on Instagram are those taken on a white background. If someone thinks they're looking at a catalogue or stock image, they'll scroll past it faster. Finding new and interesting settings for product shots should form part of your research.

2. Using story templates

Using every Instagram story feature will leave your content messy, inconsistent and amateur-looking. Story consistency and style is just as important as your feed.

In the style guide you have created, include the following parameters for your Instagram stories.

- The font or text type you use.
- The colours you use for annotations.
- How you frame images (straight, at a certain angle, etc).
- How you use and position gifs, emojis, text and annotations.
- If you know a certain picture is to be used for your story, take it in that way. Get intentional.

Try these Instagram story template apps:

Unfold and Made
For both of these apps, the free version has a selection of story templates. The premium version lets you change colours, patterns and textures as well as format video stories and unlock more backgrounds.

Canva
This app can compile Instagram story collages and videos. Within your account you can save colours, fonts and most-used shapes, for ease and consistency.

Adobe Spark
For existing Adobe Creative Suite users, test out Spark to easily and effectively add images and graphics to templates with pre-made sizing and effects.

Even when using apps, consistency rules apply. Stick to the same few effects at first, then adapt the style slowly over time. Your stories should be synonymous with your brand and recognisable at a glance.

3. Use hashtags for research

Within Instagram you can search and follow hashtags.

When searching, you will see the top posts shared using that hashtag, followed by *all* the posts shared using that hashtag.

Following hashtags will mean the top posts from these hashtags appear automatically on your feed. Be aware that your followed hashtags are public, so choose with care.

To gather ideas for content, search the hashtags most associated with your brand and look at which posts perform best. This will give an insight into the content people love to engage with within that field. For each post you see, think about why it has been so popular. Consider timing, positioning, framing, hashtagging and captioning.

Your hashtag research will help you:

- ◂ take inspiration and emulate themes

- ◂ better position or caption your posts

- ◂ spark ideas for future content

- ◂ find non-competing accounts within your field, for collaborations

- ◂ see which other hashtags these posts use, for more hashtag ideas

- ◂ learn and keep adapting your approach.

4. Test out new features

Instagram regularly rolls out new features in order to:

- ◀ stay relevant and interesting to its users
- ◀ stay relevant and useful to advertisers
- ◀ create higher barriers to entry for another social network taking its place.

Portray your brand as innovative, creative and ahead of the curve by testing out Instagram's newest features soon after they arrive. Doing this well helps position you as influential and aspirational.

STAY UP TO DATE WITH CHANGES

- ◀ Within your Instagram account, change your email settings to subscribe to updates from Instagram, so you hear about new features before others do.

- ◀ Set up a Google Alert for 'Instagram new feature' so you hear commentary from news sites on new features and how they can be used.

- ◀ Keep an eye on Instagram stories that come from Instagram. They are often used to launch new features and give guidance on usage.

- ◀ Subscribe to YouTube channels that specifically discuss Instagram. Once a new feature is announced, they will explore and document it as quickly as possible. Benefit from their research and apply it to your own efforts.

When you hear about a new feature, do some research into how it has been used, to get some ideas. Then look at the content you have coming up, for an opportunity to test it out.

Assess the response you receive and use that to decide if you should incorporate this new feature into future posts or stories. Ask for feedback from your trusted followers.

5. Check out relevant brands and influencers for inspiration

Other accounts on Instagram can act as a great source of inspiration. Similar brands with similar audiences to yours provide you with information about the kind of content that's likely to be effective for you. These could be competitor brands, collaborators, influencers or just brands you like.

Keep an eye on the people and accounts whose content and communities you aspire towards. Take inspiration from their content ideas, themes and images.

◀ Make a list of the accounts worth following.

◀ Follow these people (not necessarily your competitors).

◀ Write down the learning points and ideas.

◀ Get critical. Imagine this was your feed. What would you change?

◀ Incorporate the learning into your own posts.

◀ Schedule frequent checks.

◀ Listen out for whenever you hear someone mention an account they like, and add them to your list.

Make notes on the following:

◀ Their image and video types, including the composition, frequency, theming and colour palettes.

◀ Their use of captioning and the tone they portray.

◀ Their use of hashtags, locations and tagging of others.

◀ The images they have been tagged in.

◀ Any trends in their most popular posts, either in terms of likes or comments.

As your account gathers traction and grows, others will use it for their own inspiration, too.

6. Pinterest

At first, finding ideas might seem difficult, but soon they'll come naturally and you'll be posting effortlessly. To get well and truly in the zone of creating great content, you need to immerse yourself in great content, and one way of doing this is to use Pinterest.

Pinterest calls itself a search engine rather than a social network and this might be right. You can search for any given phrase and see pages upon pages of images relating to that term. Pinterest will sort them based on relevancy and popularity, which gives rise to high-quality images that people like to look at – perfect for Instagram!

1. List five or six themes that define your brand, product or services.
2. Sign up to Pinterest.
3. Change your privacy settings so that your account and boards are private.
4. In the search bar, type the themes in one by one.
5. Scroll down the images you see, looking for those you like the look of; those with aspects that you could emulate; those that you could easily recreate with your brand.
6. Click 'save' on the images fitting these criteria and name the board 'Ideas for Instagram'.

Use Pinterest to gather ideas for:
- new and interesting ways you could display your products in Instagram posts
- ideas for a photoshoot
- colour schemes, lighting and photograph effects
- camera angles to try out
- creating a visual brief to give to a photographer or designer.

You can also collaborate on Pinterest boards, to share your inspiration with your Instagram teammates or suppliers.

7. Quick-fire content ideas

For that extra dose of inspiration, here are some ideas we love. Choose those that are relevant to your brand.

INSTAGRAM STORIES

- Film a panning shot of your current location, with the text or hashtag 'today's office', 'behind the scenes' or 'where the magic happens'.

- Host an AMA (ask me anything). Use the Instagram story sticker that lets someone ask you a question, then respond via subsequent stories. You do not have to answer every question you are asked and you can seed questions from your friends to get it started.

- Test ideas for posts. Upload an image to your story then use the poll feature to ask a question about it. Use the response to dictate your post content.

- Share a teaser of a new product or piece of content you're going to be launching or sharing soon.

- Promote your latest posts by sending them to your story.

- Make use of collateral you already have by editing down a longer video to share a snippet on your story.

- Share reviews or testimonials – these might look too self-promotional as posts, but stories are perfect for highlighting them.

- Tips and tricks might be easy to share as a story and could add value for your audience.

- Host an interview with a key person in your industry.

- Share a 'click to reveal' combination of images.

INSTAGRAM POSTS

- ✈ Celebrate a birthday or company milestone – people will get involved to say congratulations and show they care.

- ✈ Post an inspirational quote that's relevant to your brand or current situation, or a thought-leadership quote from yourself or your brand's CEO.

- ✈ Post a quick snap of the team or people you're with.

- ✈ Post an answer to an FAQ or something you think your audience might want to know.

- ✈ Repost something about your brand that was shared by a fan or collaborator.

- ✈ Post a flatlay of your products, today's desk or what's in your bag.

- ✈ Share a 'swipe to reveal' combination of images, either revealing more info or the answer to a question with every swipe.

- ✈ Feature just one single product and make it look and sound awesome.

- ✈ Share a relevant meme. Just make sure it fits with your brand.

Chapter Three
Community

The word 'community' is an important one for Instagram. Your community is more than just your followers, because it includes the people you reach *and* the people in your audience. Instagram accounts that are active in building a community rather than just a large following are far more influential in their sector and as a brand.

Your community likely shares common values, interests and attitudes and being able to communicate these within online networks deepens your relationships within them. Building trust and rapport with your audience is a multi-level endeavour that goes beyond branding and content.

What community means

Every niche and sub-niche on Instagram has a community. For example, there's a fitness community and a vegan community. There's also a vegan fitness community. So every Instagram account will almost certainly operate within several communities, some broad, some very niche.

It is also possible to build a community around your own specific brand. This is somewhat easier for well-known brands, celebrity accounts or simply very large accounts. These accounts are almost a niche in themselves because people might identify strongly as being fans. (Ever see someone with a Harley Davidson or an Ironman tattoo?) However, it is possible for you to develop some of the benefits of a community built around your brand and that's what we're going to look at here.

Why a community matters

The vast majority of the largest accounts on Instagram are personal, rather than brand-based. This shows how important the human side of social media is.

Yet businesses play a significant role on the platform, and some key stats from Instagram are worth considering.

◀ One-third of the most-viewed Instagram stories are from businesses.

◀ 60 per cent of users say they discover new products on Instagram.

◀ 200 million+ users visit at least one business profile every day.

Brand accounts are not as popular or numerous as personal accounts but they clearly benefit from using Instagram. Integrating your brand account into communities is the way to bridge the brand–person gap and build meaningful relationships, demonstrating shared values and interests with the individuals in your audience.

Interaction is a skill

Interaction with other accounts is one of the primary ways of taking part in or building a community. Remember that your Instagram account is not a museum or a view-only exhibit; it's an interactive place. You want to make people feel welcome. It's a skill to be able to strike up an engaging and worthwhile conversation and develop a relationship using only text and emojis.

Communities are not built overnight; they are the sum of consistent and intentional actions over time. Developing the right habits of interaction will help you regularly engage your audience and increase your reach.

Superfans

There is a marketing concept devised by Kevin Kelly which asserts that if a brand can create a core network of 1,000 true fans, these individuals will help market your brand for you and you will have a viable business.

This concept works especially well for social media, where you're seeking die-hard followers that will help to share content and with initial traction. These individuals are also likely to share information about your brand, recommend you to their own networks and present you with opportunities.

These superfans have become so because of the experience they've had with your brand. Maybe they know you personally, or perhaps they resonate deeply with your message, were one of your first customers or have been consistently happy with their purchases. They're loyal and totally onboard with everything your brand does.

Not everyone in your community will be a superfan, but your actions over time will help convert more or find them from outside your current network. In general, building your overall presence will increase its value over time. If you've ever heard the saying 'Your network is your net worth', it's surely applicable to Instagram.

The four steps to building a community

This chapter is split into the following four areas:

1. Understanding Your Community
2. Active Outreach
3. Responding to Engagement
4. Encouraging Interaction

Understanding Your Community

Having a deeper understanding of your existing network is the basis for growing and evolving it. You may find nuggets of information and surprising trends that will assist you in making a deeper connection with them.

Active Outreach

Instagram provides brands with a plethora of tactics to find and reach out to new audience members.

Responding to Engagement

A well-executed content strategy will yield post engagement. How you respond to this can heavily influence the reach of a post as well as the relationships it creates.

Encouraging Interaction

Knowing the value of post engagement and audience interaction, we explore the ways to increase the volume. Posts that start conversations can be the most beneficial to brands expanding their community because they create more opportunities to use all of the tactics discussed in this section.

Understanding Your Community

The first step to aligning yourself with your audience is to know them inside out. This isn't just knowing stats about their gender or average age; it's understanding their interests, their daily habits, their hopes and fears and much more. Of course, some of the finer holistic details are hard to determine with statistics alone, so a range of tactics is required.

Knowledge is power

In the digital age, there is so much information available to you. The more you know about your audience, the better you can resonate with them and the more your community can grow. Some companies invest heavily in audience insights, such as:

- conducting surveys
- hosting focus groups
- behaviour-monitoring tools
- mystery shopping/dining
- A/B testing on all kinds of print and digital media.

Their findings have a huge bearing on the way they position their brand and their messaging.

Yet understanding your community goes beyond the basic attributes of your target audience. Your audience may already be well defined by the services or products you provide. For example, you may have a very specific niche in terms of the demographic and income bracket of your following. However, in reaching and influencing these individuals, it's just as important to know what they follow: the brands, influencers and other accounts.

This kind of intuitive and qualitative information can be equally valuable to the raw data, especially when trying to create an emotional buy-in from your community.

Being exclusive

Knowing your audience well enables you to tailor your presence to them and only them. Your brand must be proudly exclusive to your audience. You've taken the time to learn about them and appreciate what they want to see and hear; it's time to leverage that. The more niche and specific you are, the more likely you are to generate a meaningful connection.

Be the best version of you

It's important that your brand is aspirational to your community. You want to be the 'must follow' account within the communities of interest to you and your audience should want to align themselves with you. However, it's important that you remain true to what your brand represents.

Authenticity is paramount. If you're pretending to be something you're not, it's incredibly difficult to keep up the act. Avoid saying anything online that you wouldn't say in real life and don't get involved in discussions you don't have any passion for. Connect with your audience members by finding common ground, not looking to be divisive. These considerations make being the best version of you in Instagram a balancing act, especially in the long term.

Community and the algorithm

Two very important elements of the Instagram algorithm are 'interest' and 'relationship'. By keeping your account relevant to your audience and deepening your relationship with them, you'll increase your reach and influence.

We're going to look at ten methods that will give you a better understanding of your audience.

1. Find out which accounts your audience follow

The first step in building your community is understanding it. You can learn a lot from the accounts your followers follow.

The list of who someone follows is public, as long as their account is set to public, which means they will likely follow accounts they want to be associated with. These are the people your audience wants to engage with and this is the type of content they want to see.

CHECK THEM OUT

1. Locate a follower and click on their account.

2. Click 'Following'.

3. Look through the list of the hashtags and accounts they follow.

At the top of the list will be the accounts you have in common; those that you also follow. Viewing mutual connections provides a valuable insight in to the circles this person is in.

Use this information to glean further insights about your audience and their interests. Become familiar with the people in your community and the other people and brands they look to for inspiration. You might be surprised by the breadth of accounts within your niche and extended network and discover some unlikely crossovers.

2. Find out when your audience is online and active

By now you should be aware of which times of day are best for you to post content, based on how much engagement you receive from different update times. Go one step further by finding out when your audience is online.

Popular accounts receive constant notifications, and Instagram limits the number that appear on the 'Activity' tab. For best engagement results and a greater chance of response, interact with someone's account when they are online.

Business accounts can use Instagram insights and the 'Audience' section to see when their audience is most active. The 'Audience' tab also displays the most popular days of the week for your audience. Accounts with a business focus, for example, may be far busier on weekdays than weekends. Or you may see consistent activity, regardless of the day. This information should form part of your interaction calendar.

The most popular time of day is likely early morning and evening in the time zone of your target audience. If your followers are based in more than one time zone, the insights will reflect this. For example, for an account with followers split between the UK and the USA, the busiest time is likely to be the early evening in the UK, which is the morning across the USA.

Study the most active times displayed. This is when your community-building efforts will be most effective because at these times your followers are likely to see your outreach straight away.

3. Identify common trends in bios

The information contained within the bios of your audience provides valuable insights with which to inform your conversations and outreach.

An Instagram bio gives someone 160 characters to explain their work, life and purpose to a stranger. It's everything they want the world to know about them at a glance, so you can bet they've thought about it carefully. This information is important to them so it should be important to you as well.

Look through the bios of your followers and notice trends in the following areas:

- ◂ The main focus of their account (work, family, hobbies, food, etc).
- ◂ Words they use to describe themselves (entrepreneur, mum, athlete, writer, etc).
- ◂ How they use their bio link (personal website, blog, shop page, etc).

Use the information gathered to write a word cloud of the themes you find. This is what your audience cares about. Notice common areas of interest with your own account and make a note of themes they cover that you don't. These new topics are peripheral to your core content.

Next, look through their accounts and notice trends in the following areas:

- ◂ How influential their accounts are (follower count, engagement, number of story highlights).
- ◂ How image-conscious they are (edited images, optimised account, graphic design, filters and consistent theming).
- ◂ The focus of their images (scenes, themselves, activities, kids, words, hobbies, etc).
- ◂ How they communicate (tone of voice, emojis, length of captions, call to action).

4. Follow accounts that you want to be your audience

Within your industry, identify the Instagram accounts of other key players, those names that are synonymous with your sector and what you represent. These are perfect accounts for you to follow for a number of reasons.

1. Following them first increases the chance of them following you back. Some Instagram accounts will follow back those that follow them first, which means your account grows.

2. It will increase your association with those people and position you firmly within that industry. Their followers will be able to see your username on posts that you like and in their list of followers.

3. You will regularly see their content and develop more relevant ideas of your own.

4. Instagram's algorithm may start to learn that you're a key person in that community, which means you may be suggested to others as a person to follow.

5. It's expected. You hope that experts in other fields keep up to date with industry news, updates and key players. It's the same for you.

WHO SHOULD YOU FOLLOW?
Follow well-known speakers, business people, influencers, authors and professionals in your chosen niche. Follow people you admire and whose work you take inspiration from. Avoid anyone who doesn't fit your vibe or whose content would annoy you.

5. Engage with other posts just before you post

Instagram's algorithm is shrouded in mystery. We know that Instagram prioritises feed posts by your friends, family and people you regularly engage with and tests suggest that interaction with other accounts just before you post makes your post more likely to be shown to your followers.

With this in mind, plan your active engagement time each week to happen just before or just after you post an update of your own. Your new post might be higher up in the feeds of your followers as a result of your recent interaction.

Even if this suspected algorithm boost isn't true, engaging in active outreach before you post might mean that someone who has a notification from you looks at your posts. They might then reciprocate the engagement on your most recent one.

This is applicable no matter how many followers you have. All accounts can benefit from an algorithm boost to keep engagement high and all accounts benefit from more eyes on their most recent post.

6. Follow the followers of accounts similar to yours

Now you have identified the speakers, business people, influencers, authors and professionals in your chosen niche, check out their followers.

Someone who follows an account similar to yours is likely to want to follow you too; your posts will focus on similar themes as you belong to the same niche. Alert these accounts to your presence by following them first. They can then choose to check out your posts or follow you back.

In practice:

1. Find four or five accounts as similar to yours as possible, ideally with a slightly larger following.

2. Look at their followers and find those that match your own target audience.

3. Follow some of them.

TOP TIPS

◀ Exercise some caution. Research a variety of accounts; don't just systematically follow all of one account's followers. The goal is to take inspiration and grow your network without copying someone else's follower base.

◀ Be aware that large accounts (500k+ followers) might have a large proportion of automated accounts (bots) following them. Check out accounts to make sure they are real before you follow them. Always go for quality over quantity.

◀ Instagram has upper limits on the amount of actions, including follows, you can make within a specific time period. Make sure you know what this is before you start following numerous accounts.

7. Ask your followers what they want you to post

Get your community involved in your account by asking them what you should post about. It shows you're listening, it shows you care and it shows you're open to new ideas. It also allows you to better serve your audience and create posts that they are more likely to engage with, especially if they relate to topics they have specifically requested.

You can respond to suggestions you receive with follow-up questions and explore them further. Use any conversation as an excuse to deepen a relationship and create a superfan – it's flattering when an account you follow takes your comments on board. Amassing comments on posts and stories also has an algorithmic boost.

This takes inspiration from YouTubers, who often:

- ◄ ask for feedback on content that their audience wants to see, including suggestions of upcoming topics
- ◄ signpost that a particular video is the first content piece of its kind to see what the audience thinks. This tells an audience that their feedback is valuable in dictating future content and positions the account firmly within its user base
- ◄ ask their followers if they would like to see more of specific types of content.

Any information arising from this exercise is likely to be from your most vocal fans and followers and is valuable in understanding their needs and progressing your content. Demonstrating that you're open to suggestions also shows a vulnerability which might resonate well with your audience. We're all humans trying to serve and entertain each other.

TOP TIP Seed some comments to start the ball rolling. Private message your friends to let them know you're collecting ideas and ask them to comment.

8. Spend some time on the 'Explore' tab

According to online publisher TechCrunch, 'Half of Instagram's billion-plus users open their Explore tab each month to find fresh content and creators.'

The Explore tab can be found by clicking the search icon on your Instagram homepage. Herein lies a goldmine of information, completely tailored to your account and including ads, popular content, ideas and new people to engage with.

Your Explore tab generates content that reflects how you use the app. It's your very own echo chamber, designed to keep you on the app for longer by showing you content that Instagram is sure will spark your interest.

Here's why you should spend some time on your Explore tab.

- You will see the kind of content that Instagram thinks your account is about.
- You will see content that Instagram thinks you will like.
- You will see new accounts whose content you can follow and comment on.
- It might spark ideas for new content ideas and how you could appear on the Explore tab yourself.

The Explore tab is one of the reasons why it's important that your entire Instagram account is on-brand – even who you follow and what you engage with. Everything feeds into one algorithm and it's Instagram's way of understanding who you are.

Stick to your niche for everything you do. Keep your account completely aligned with your brand. If you're constantly searching and engaging around topic A, but you post and build your brand around topic B, there's misalignment and you're sending mixed signals to Instagram about how relevant you are within your niche.

9. Remove spam followers

While the number of followers you have is a vanity metric, it's also a good indication of how much the content and engagement you're putting out there is resonating with your target audience.

Work out your engagement rate per post by dividing the number of likes and comments by your total follower number and multiplying it by 100. An account with 3,000 followers and an average of 300 likes and comments on each post has an engagement rate of 10 per cent. Anything over 5 per cent is a sign that your content is attractive to your followers.

If your follower base consists of genuine people, you stand a better chance of your engagement rate being higher. And if your posts achieve low engagement rate, Instagram thinks your followers don't like your posts.

Check how many fake followers your account is predicted to have by entering your user name in online tools such as the 'Follower Checker' tool from Influencer Marketing Hub and the 'Influencer Lookup' tool from Mighty Scout. Most accounts have some, but ideally your account has over 80 per cent real followers.

Don't just run these tests on your own account. Check out other accounts before you begin any collaborations, to check they are as influential as they say they are. Next, go through your list of followers and see if any are obviously spam accounts. Tell-tale signs include:

- if they're following hundreds of accounts and have hardly any followers
- a lack of bio or profile picture
- if they link to somewhere spammy from their profile (don't click the link)
- if their comments on your posts are spammy or irrelevant.

Clean up your account every once in a while to keep your engagement percentage high and a true reflection of the actual activity level.

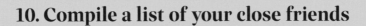

10. Compile a list of your close friends

The ability to compile a list of 'close friends' is a useful but underutilised feature on Instagram.

By adding users to your close friends list, you can post story updates that are only seen by these people and not shared via Instagram. Even better than that, a member of your close friends list will know they are seeing content designed only for them and they will know that they are on that list because the outline around your profile picture will be bright green instead of pink when there's a story ready to view.

Having a close friends list creates exclusivity around your account and let's specific people know they are special to you.

WHY YOU MIGHT UTILISE A CLOSE FRIENDS LIST

- To share exclusive content with your closest crew, or your brand's most loyal fans or customers.
- Perhaps you've planned a small event or an invitation-only gathering at a location that you don't want to share with everyone who follows you.
- If you are sharing slightly off-brand or super personal information (although here I'd question if it should be on Instagram at all).
- To focus on a specific sub-section of your audience. Perhaps your entire account is aimed at mummy bloggers, but your close friends list consists of mummy bloggers who have reviewed your product. You might like to reward them by sharing specific content only with them.

Create a close friends list by using the 'Close Friends' option in your Instagram menu, then choose who joins the list. Instagram will show you suggested members based on who it thinks you might like to add, which is a handy time-saver.

Tentsile, UK
@TENTSILE

Jess Reading, Marketing director

The photogenic nature brand whose products compel customers to share.

Tentsile grew overnight in early 2017 from a viral Facebook video posted by the influencer David Wolfe, which led to Tentsile's products selling out and the US becoming their number one market. They couldn't produce fast enough or keep up with retailer enquiries and since then the #tentsile hashtag has been used over 25,000 times. Hear how the brand has harnessed that viral phenomena ever since.

TELL ME ABOUT YOUR INSTAGRAM ACCOUNT.

We started our account in 2015 so we could, relatively quickly and cheaply, introduce our tree tents to a global audience. With such a unique product, that looks great in photographs, we knew that adventurers worldwide would want to learn about this brand new camping concept.

At the start our three main goals on Instagram were to generate awareness of our brand and products, inspire people to spend more time enjoying the outdoors, and invite customers to share their adventures and stimulate user-generated content.

WHAT DO MEMBERS OF YOUR AUDIENCE HAVE IN COMMON?

Our audience all have a love of the outdoors. They want to experience nature in a different way and share their experiences with like-minded people.

Our brand is centred around the protection of the world's trees and forests and raising the awareness of the importance of the world's forests. We'd like to think this is also something our community has in common. We work with Leave No Trace to promote outdoor camping ethics, which is one of the reasons we have such an avid and loyal audience.

HOW HAVE SALES GROWN AS YOUR COMMUNITY HAS GROWN?

Social media and particularly Instagram is an incredibly important channel for us for driving traffic to the website and generating conversions. We have over 198,000 followers on Instagram and this channel accounts for 5 per cent of our monthly sales. However, the way people shop now isn't linear. Like most brands, we have an omni-channel marketing strategy and all these channels interplay so the true impact of Instagram will be greater than what we are able to track.

HOW DO YOU ENGAGE WITH YOUR COMMUNITY?

We only post content that we think is relevant and fun and will really inspire our audience. We don't post for the sake of posting. We engage with our community without interactions being forced. We receive lots of comments to our posts, which we actively reply to and we strike up conversations with those who are interested.

We partner with other outdoor brands at least once a month to offer a giveaway, a reward for staying with us as well as to introduce new brands to our community. Based on five years of data, we have a pretty good idea of what our community want to see from us to keep them engaged.

We've maintained our 198,000 followers over several years and the people who buy our products or follow us on Instagram are genuine fans. The user-generated content they have contributed hasn't been incentivised, it's from our community's desire to actively share their experiences. They use our products in ways we'd never thought about and they capture this for everyone.

WHAT DO YOU DO EACH WEEK?

We post a minimum of three times per week and draw our content posts from newly created user-generated content as well as content from our brand ambassadors and lifestyle photography. We know which days of the week and times of the day are the best for us to post based on historical engagements and when our audience is online and active. We have an 'always on' strategy to ensure we stay relevant and in the minds of our community.

We're normally able to predict how well a post will perform. We have lots of data from over five years of experience of interacting with our audience so we instinctively know what they want to see. Sometimes we surprise ourselves when posts might not get the reaction we thought they would, but this helps us get better and learn more.

HOW HAS YOUR ACCOUNT EVOLVED OVER THE YEARS AND MONTHS?

The early days of Instagram were when we saw the best traction and our largest growth rates in followers. Everyone wanted to collaborate, there was lots of original content which large Instagram accounts wanted to use and share and influencer photographers were happy to produce and share content on a gear exchange basis. With the growth and popularity of influencers and the huge amounts of content available, this has changed the way we work on the Instagram platform. A lot of opportunities are now on a paid-for basis as everyone wants to monetise the platform. Now we focus on organic growth, harvesting user-generated content and collaborating with young, aspiring photographers.

OUR AUDIENCE ALL HAVE A LOVE OF THE OUTDOORS. THEY WANT TO EXPERIENCE NATURE IN DIFFERENT WAYS AND SHARE THEIR ADVENTURES WITH LIKE-MINDED PEOPLE.

WE ONLY POST CONTENT THAT WE THINK IS RELEVANT AND FUN AND WILL REALLY INSPIRE OUR AUDIENCE, AND WE DON'T POST FOR THE SAKE OF POSTING.

Active Outreach

The interactive element of social media is what makes it social – the instant, public, two-way communication between brands and individuals creates a revolutionary marketing channel. Brands can make the first move when it comes to B2C communications, which opens doors for creativity and develops deeper and more meaningful customer relationships.

Types of interaction

Audience interaction can be broadly categorised into two types: proactive and reactive. The distinction is in how the interaction was initiated, whether by the consumer (reactive from the brand's perspective) or by the brand (proactive).

Community management and customer service are generally reactive, in that brands are responding to inbound communications. This makes for a rather passive approach to interaction as it simply doesn't happen unless someone else makes the first move.

Active outreach is the opposite. Here, brands seek opportunities to start conversations, or at least get involved in them. Some of the greatest social media wins for brands happen when they capitalise on these kinds of opportunities.

You don't have to set out to try and make a viral comment or start a movement; each interaction is a contribution to your community. Making one person smile or think differently is a win, but the likelihood is you'll influence differing numbers of people based on the nature of the interaction.

Counteracting negativity

If your brand handles negative comments or even complaints online, having positive conversations on Instagram can help redress the balance.

If businesses are seen only responding to complaints, this might create a generally negative or defensive tone to their Instagram account. Being proactive and starting the conversation first means you set the tone.

If you can find individuals, whether they follow you or not, who are in some way relevant to your brand, you can certainly sway the sentiment and increase the number of positive exchanges your account has. You may find more people come to your defence in the future or that it simply works as a distraction tactic.

How Instagram beats Facebook

The ability to reach out proactively to consumers is a huge benefit of Instagram versus Facebook. Both are excellent content platforms, but Facebook doesn't permit business pages to contact users unless the individual initiates a conversation with the page.

Much like Twitter, Instagram is far more open in terms of interaction, which in some ways makes them examples of true social networks. They give you the potential to find your customers and open discussions. This is a form of 'social listening' and it's where smaller, more savvy brands on Instagram can build valuable relationships.

It doesn't have to be people specifically talking about your brand or product that means you can get involved in conversations. We'll explore nine different options available, some of which may be a goldmine of opportunity.

1. Use hashtags to search Instagram

You can use hashtags to search for users, as well as to help users find your content. Create a list of hashtags to search regularly to find accounts to interact with.

My agency represents a well-known restaurant group which uses unique names for their menu items. Searching for these items as Instagram hashtags brings up their customers' images, which we can then comment on and start conversations about. This allows the group to develop customer relations outside the restaurants.

FIND YOUR AUDIENCE USING HASHTAGS

◀ If you're a local business, search for local area place names. Think in groups of hyperlocal, local, then national hashtags: #Kihei, #Maui, #Hawaii; or #Harborne, #Birmingham, #UnitedKingdom; or #GreenPoint, #CapeTown, #SouthAfrica, and so on. (I just hashtagged these terms on a trip and had Maui tour groups messaging and commenting on my posts.)

◀ If you're an online business, think about your products or services and what someone might hashtag. For example, for pet ecommerce, look for #newpuppy, #mydog, #lovemydog, #instadog. For virtual PA services, look for #businessowner, #entrepreneur, #employer.

◀ If you're a blogger or influencer, try searching for hashtags that fit your niche: #fitness, #fitfam, #weightlifter; or #foodie, #foodblogger, #paleo.

TOP TIP Stuck? Start by running searches on the hashtags you use for your own content.

Compile your list of hashtags and start engaging. See it as trial and error. You're finding out which hashtags connect you to the right people and how receptive they are.

Test out different types of message: super friendly versus more direct; with and without emojis; personalised versus more general. If in doubt, stay away from being too salesy, and just be friendly, inclusive and positive.

2. Actively engage with the people you follow

Throughout the week, take time to scroll your feed to see posts from accounts and hashtags you follow. Instagram's algorithm reorders posts based on what it thinks you want to see, and it intersperses posts with ads, which means you might need to scroll for a while to see a good variety of posts.

Being an active member of your community means engaging with these posts and reciprocating any engagement they have given. Liking someone's post means they see a notification from you. It means they refamiliarise themselves with your profile picture, username and perhaps your account or stories if they click to view further and it shows you've taken the time to pay them attention.

Research shows that the more familiar something becomes, the more we like and trust it. If someone regularly sees your name or brand name, it has the same effect. Backed up with consistent and high-quality content, this positions your brand at the forefront of your audience's mind.

Before social media, brands could only have in-person interactions, spend a fortune on billboard or TV ads, or rely on word of mouth conversations that they weren't a part of. In comparison, actively engaging with people you follow online is a cost-effective way of reaching people.

Incorporate scrolling and double tapping posts on your feed into your weekly plan.

3. Personalise your comments

Commenting on posts goes one step beyond liking them, but what it lacks in efficiency it makes up for in effect. Comment in a specific and personalised way on the posts of people you follow, as well as new users you find through hashtag or location searches.

Personalising your comments means that the recipient knows you're not an automated bot (there are many on Instagram) and that you have taken the time to look at their post and add something personal to create a more valuable connection.

Even a small Instagram account might receive hundreds of likes on one of their posts, but only a few comments. Therefore your comment is more likely to be noticed, by the user and their other followers. It's more likely to spark further conversation and have the community-building effect desired.

TOP TIPS

- Be specific and direct.

- Be positive and happy.

- Read the comment back and check it can't be misinterpreted.

- Ask yourself, 'What would I think if someone wrote this on my post?'.

4. Respond to people's stories

Responding to the Instagram stories of people you follow is more personal than liking and commenting on posts as your response is private. This is how you 'slide into someone's DMs', as the phrase goes. This means they will receive a direct message (DM) notification. DMs are traditionally reserved for close friends, so you'll be in there with them.

Story responses let someone know you have seen their post and taken the time to engage with it. You don't even need to type a comment. When you view stories and tap the comment box you will usually be shown a selection of emojis to click on. Clicking one 'reacts' to the user's story and they receive a DM to tell them you have done so.

Unless someone takes a screen shot and shares your message, other people can't see what you have written; however, you should still only give appropriate responses and make sure you don't say anything you wouldn't want spreading further.

TO INTERACT USING STORIES

- ◄ Scroll to the top of your Instagram app and click on the first story.
- ◄ Tap the comment box and either choose an appropriate emoji or write a comment.
- ◄ Go to the next story and repeat. And repeat. Instagram will keep showing you Instagram stories as long as you keep tapping.
- ◄ Set a timer so you don't go on forever.

The least salesy way of using story interaction is as a casual conversation starter – giving a compliment or saying well done. More salesy ways include sharing discount codes and product, event or company information, but wait until you're into a conversation before doing that. You could also start a conversation by asking a question in your story response.

5. Tag people in your comments

When posting your content you will already have tagged any relevant people, brands and places in your post. However, you might also want specific people, who aren't within the post, to see this content. Tagging someone in a comment is the same as sending it directly to them, but in a more public way.

MAKING USE OF TAGGING

◀ If you see something on Instagram that you know a member of your community will find funny or interesting, tag them in a comment. It shows you're thinking of them and it's a nice compliment.

◀ Use Instagram comments to link members of your audience together. Make introductions, draw similarities and give them an excuse to connect. It demonstrates your understanding of their accounts and they're more likely to reciprocate.

◀ Tag your friends, family and members of your team when you see inspiration for photoshoots, destinations, products, or anything else relevant to your account and business. Help them understand your creative ideas and know what to look out for.

◀ Perhaps you have a new follower and you'd like them to see a summary post that will help them understand you and your brand, for example. Tagging them serves as an introduction and welcomes them to your account.

6. Send disappearing DMs

Disappearing DMs is where Instagram meets Snapchat. Instagram is roughly three times the size of Snapchat, yet the two are still regularly compared and have very similar features.

Instagram's direct messaging function lets you share voice notes and videos that can be viewed or listened to once, then they disappear. They can be sent either as a group or individual message.

When sending a disappearing photo or video, you can:

◀ select 'View Once' to let the person or group receiving your photo or video view it once

◀ select 'Allow Replay' to loop your photo or video and to let the recipient open and replay your photo or video one more time before it disappears

◀ select 'Keep in Chat' to keep a preview image of the photo or video visible in the chat thread.

Use this strategy to give exclusive behind the scenes shots, exciting new information, or to disclose news reserved only for your most loyal fans. For example, a store opening, a product launch, sneak peeks, hints at the future, and so on.

GET CREATIVE

◀ Surprise a follower by recording a personal voice note for them.

◀ Design your image or video so that it flashes up on the screen quickly, so if you blink you'll miss it.

◀ Run a quiz using this method, whereby entrants need to play a message once then submit their answer to win prizes.

7. Follow active accounts

Be choosy about who you follow. Treat it like an exclusive club and don't give away membership lightly. Your Instagram account is more valuable if your following and followers are active on the platform.

One way to keep your account selective is to run quarterly checks for inactive accounts. Inactive accounts don't like, comment or share on Instagram, but following them affects your follow ratio.

An inactive account is one that hasn't posted in 30, 60 or 90 days (they may have stopped using Instagram, for example). Some third-party apps – including FindUnfollow or Cleaner for IG – identify the inactive accounts you're following so that you can unfollow them.

TOP TIPS

◄ As well as following inactive accounts, think about unfollowing accounts that are too active. If your feed is filled with one account posting multiple times a day, you could unfollow them to allow accounts to appear more prominently on your feed.

◄ If you do use a third-party app, check that it complies with Instagram's policy and be careful with your password.

8. Organise power hours of interaction

Add regular interaction to your Instagram diary, ideally just before or after you post on your feed, incorporating all the interaction methods we've looked at so far:

◄ hashtag searches

◄ liking feed posts

◄ following users

◄ commenting on feed posts

◄ story responses, emojis and messages

◄ disappearing DMs

◄ tagging people in comments.

Keep your interaction manageable by scheduling power hours at specific times each week; you'll glean better data if your activity is at consistent times.

Keep track of how much you do in your power hour one week and use that to inform what you do with the next sprint.

Mix up the methods. Split your power hour between two interactions from the list above, allocating 30 minutes for each, then focus on two different methods in the following session. Work out which interaction method is the most effective use of your time. And be aware of the engagement you receive in response to your outreach; get a feel for what generates the most buzz.

TOP TIP Instagram's has restrictions on how many actions an account can make, normally over a 60-minute period. If you're really on a roll, you might start to behave like a bot, or you might violate Instagram's usage policies. Check the most recent limits before you begin and make sure you don't hit them for happy interacting that's within the rules.

9. Regram or reshare others' posts

Sharing the post of another Instagram account is one of the highest compliments you can give. It suggests you are aligned with that account and it keeps you in contact with someone over and above liking and commenting.

You're also doing them a favour because their post will be seen by more people, including potential new followers in your audience. And it might mean that they're more likely to reciprocate and share your content. Generate even more content you can share by encouraging others to tag you in posts and letting them know why.

Sharing others' posts also serves as a fresh way of coming up with content. Share posts that:

- use the hashtags associated with your brand
- people you follow have shared that is also appropriate for your audience
- have been created by your customers or fans and include your products or locations
- will add value or inspire your audience in some way.

You can share posts to your feed using the Regram app, which adds an attribution mark and copies the caption. Alternatively, share posts to your story using the 'Add Post To Your Story' option below each post sent from a public account. You could annotate the story with your own comments, emojis or gifs, too.

Remember: sharing is caring!

TOP TIP Ensure you give proper credit and be prepared to remove a post if someone doesn't want you to regram. This isn't about stealing someone's creativity, it's about helping to promote them.

CASE STUDY
In 2014, Dubai's tourism board came up with a #MyDubai campaign, to encourage locals and visitors to use the #MyDubai hashtag in their post. The tourism board's account would then share the best images on their own account, plus the images were searched by local businesses looking to engage with potential customers. The campaign amassed 1 million posts in six months (reference), not to mention the hours of content creation time it saved.

Responding to Engagement

All forms of engagement are invaluable to your Instagram account, because they help your profile reach more people through the impact on the algorithm. In addition, post engagements, as well as other mentions on the platform, provide opportunities to garner more influence and build your community.

Post likes are the lowest denomination in terms of public engagement and there's not a huge amount you can do with them. However, there are many other forms of engagement:

1. Post comments
2. People sharing your posts (via a regram or to their story)
3. Private messages
4. People using your hashtags
5. People mentioning your brand or sharing images of your brand
6. People tagging themselves at your locations
7. People tagging you in their posts or comments

The seven engagements listed above give you the chance to continue a conversation with the individual that has engaged with you. Someone choosing to interact with your post represents an opportunity with that person.

There are two more types of engagement. With these, you will know the number of times it happened but you won't know specifically who carried out the action:

8. People sharing your posts with their friends in direct messages
9. People saving your posts to look at later

Creating great content and a brand worthy of these nine types of engagement is the hardest part. Generating likes is easy in comparison because they just require someone to double tap their screen. Compelling someone to type a comment, mention your brand in some of their own content, or share with a friend is far more valuable.

Continue the conversation

You posted something to your feed to potentially thousands of people. That's a one-to-many kind of communication or broadcast. One of these people has now made the first move to make this a one-to-one conversation. Often people do these things in the hope of a response from you, so it's an open invitation and a chance to develop a relationship.

These conversations can elevate loyalty and influence users to take the next steps in their relationship with you. Perhaps you can convince them to make a purchase or a repeat purchase. Perhaps they'll become a superfan.

Adopt a policy

As you work through this section, it's important to think about how your brand responds to incoming engagements. Create a policy you can stick to for all of your interactions. Write it down and revisit it regularly. This will give you consistency and a way to assess your approach over the medium and long term.

Decide what you do and don't respond to. You don't want someone to feel ignored when everyone else has been answered. It's similar to how you may have policies for customer engagement in real life. How do you greet people who enter your business, buy from you, send a support ticket or enquire? There are similar categories of Instagram engagement to consider.

1. Respond positively to comments to encourage more of the same

No one likes to feel ignored. Whenever someone posts or writes something on social media they are, effectively, putting themselves out there in the hope that someone responds.

Make your audience happy by acknowledging their efforts. When you receive comments, respond. Take the time to:

- thank someone for their comment
- return a compliment
- further the conversation
- respond with an emoji.

Each notification someone receives from you builds familiarity with your brand. Responding to all comments ensures your account looks friendly and approachable and encourages more people to interact. It shows you've taken the time to nurture your community.

Consistency in responding is also important. Start from the top and acknowledge all of the comments you receive, even if the response is short. If your posts amass hundreds of comments, you could choose to respond only to those that ask a question, or you could post your own comment to say thank you and tag usernames in your response. Make your own personal policy and stick to it without exception.

You can also 'like' comments by clicking the heart to the right of the text. This will send a notification to the comment writer and show that their contribution has been acknowledged.

TOP TIP Develop a signature response, perhaps using a specific on-brand emoji, so that your audience starts to associate you with that sign.

2. Respond as quickly as possible

After you post, stay on Instagram and monitor the response. This enables you to:

- ◀ respond quickly to any comments, which might encourage more comments or live conversations in comment threads

- ◀ carry out active interaction

- ◀ check that nothing is escalating in the comments on your post

- ◀ be online when others are, gleaning insights about their Instagram behaviour and strengthening your data for when your audience is active

- ◀ answer questions requiring a personal response via direct message (DM), letting the person know you've done so.

The first 30–60 minutes after posting is paramount, as Instagram decides how many more feeds or Explore tabs to serve the post to. Use this time to maximise your live interaction and ensure your account is busy.

3. Make other people feel good

In any activity you undertake on Instagram, don't forget that behind every comment, post and account is a real person. Tone can only ever be inferred and it's easy to misinterpret meaning.

Share positively and comment compassionately. Take every opportunity to be kind. You don't have to be inauthentic, but as the saying goes, 'If you don't have anything nice to say, don't say anything at all.'

No one likes a troll, so don't be one. Feel sympathy for the trolls who try to promote negativity, but absolutely don't feed them.

Instagram is a carefully edited showreel of how people want the world to see them. Rarely can any good come from putting someone down or treating them with anything other than kindness and respect. Never embarrass or ridicule, even in jest.

Even celebrities known for their abrasiveness share and engage positively on Instagram:

- Ricky Gervais's comedy and television work often involves him ridiculing and making fun of celebrities, but he uses his Instagram to wish his community well, share behind-the-scenes pictures and tell the world how much he loves animals.

- James Blunt has made headlines through his scathing yet hilarious quips in response to online trolls on Twitter, yet he uses his Instagram to share family pictures, wish people happy holidays and generally have fun.

4. Make a plan for spammy comments

You only need to google 'Instagram comments' to see hundreds of news articles on well intended comments that were completely misinterpreted. Comments start threads and for some accounts it can get out of hand.

YOUR COMMENT OPTIONS

- ◀ **Leave the comment there and don't respond.** Do this when you receive generic comments, emoji comments, or comments you don't understand.
- ◀ **Respond with a message.** When someone asks a question or leaves a heartfelt or personal (positive) comment.
- ◀ **Respond and move the conversation to DM.** This is helpful for customer service issues or when someone asks a question you want to respond to in a less public place.
- ◀ **Like the comment.** Do this in response to a short positive comment such as 'nice work', 'great pic' or 'well done'.
- ◀ **Report the comment.** You can use Instagram's options to report spam or inappropriate comments.
- ◀ **Delete the comment.** Do this if someone has posted something you don't want others to see. However, exercise caution here. Instagram won't tell them their comment has been deleted, but they might notice and increase their activity, so do consider this before acting.

Instagram is constantly working on making its platform a safe place to be. Since 2016, it has offered a filter that removes comments featuring words and phrases it deems offensive. In 2017, this was upgraded to an AI system that takes the context of the response into consideration.

In Instagram's 'Comment Controls' menu you can choose to automatically hide comments that may be offensive. You can also manually add words and phrases of your own and Instagram will hide comments that contain them.

You could also choose to only allow comments from your followers and people you follow. Or turn off comments altogether in the option menu for each individual post.

Frenchiestore, USA
@FRENCHIESTORE

Sunny Oshan, Founder

The ethical pet brand building a niche community to grow their ecommerce business.

Sunny started her Instagram account in 2015, initially to share custom artworks she made for people and their dogs. She also used to share pictures and videos of French bulldogs, her favourite breed.

Now Frenchiestore is a Shopify website selling pet accessories for dog health, safety and style. The community includes over 134,000 current or aspiring pet parents.

WHAT WERE YOUR GOALS? AT THE START AND CURRENTLY?

My goals were to build a community of dog lovers all around the world, that support each other, and this goal has not changed with time. However, new goals have emerged, like providing dogs with health-conscious pet products. With our big following comes great responsibility.

HOW DO YOU ENGAGE WITH YOUR COMMUNITY?

Frenchiestore was founded and built on values of love and care for our dog community. Engagement and keeping strong personal ties with our community is extremely important to us.

Each year when we launch our new line of pyjamas we run an Instagram 'cyber pyjama party'. Our supporters all post pictures of their dogs in their pyjamas to let the dog community know, and they use our Frenchiestore hashtag. We do Instagram giveaways regularly, especially during the holidays. Giveaways are a great way to build engagement and have other people learn about our brand.

We also have a closed and private Instagram DM group with members who are personally invited by us. Those members include our most loyal representatives. In this group we talk daily, discussing design and event ideas. They have early access to new items before public release.

Our audience is very loyal, partly because of the personal attention I give them over Instagram. Whenever they send a message they receive a prompt and personal response from me, which they appreciate. As the owner of the business I am able to answer any questions directly and quickly.

ARE YOU ABLE TO TRACK SALES FROM INSTAGRAM TO YOUR STORE?

Yes. Our website platform is Shopify, which allows me to track every detail of a sale, including the number of orders someone has placed, how many visits they made over what period of time and how they found our website. It's really useful for us to see how Instagram contributes to sales.

WHAT DO YOU DO EACH WEEK?

We post three or four times daily. We feature most of our new customers, repeating customers, representatives and breeders on our feed. In our experience, posting once a day is not nearly enough. We have done this since the very beginning. In addition, we repost stories when accounts tag us, and we never miss a story. We use the same hashtags related to our niche of the French bulldog breed. We also use hashtags related to our products, such as #noplastic.

We also post news that could potentially help other pet parents, as well as ongoing updates as they emerge. People come to our page because they know they will find helpful and current information.

CAN YOU PREDICT HOW WELL A POST WILL DO BEFORE YOU POST IT?

I can somewhat predict how well a post will do. A post with a Frenchie breed dog on my page performs better than when I post a different breed. A video that provokes a positive emotion will do better than a photo post, and puppy pictures and videos always do better than product posts that don't feature dogs.

DO YOU HAVE KNOWLEDGE OF INSTAGRAM'S ALGORITHM?

I believe the algorithm favours brands that tag products and appear in the shopping section, accounts that gained popularity faster than others, and people using new updated features.

Today, instead of trying to get a 'viral' video, the way to grow organically is through word of mouth and micro influencers. There are no shortcuts on Instagram.

OUR AUDIENCE IS VERY LOYAL, PARTLY BECAUSE OF THE PERSONAL ATTENTION I GIVE THEM OVER INSTAGRAM. WHENEVER THEY SEND A MESSAGE THEY RECEIVE A PROMPT AND PERSONAL RESPONSE FROM ME.

FRENCHIESTORE WAS FOUNDED AND BUILT ON VALUES OF LOVE AND CARE FOR OUR DOG COMMUNITY. ENGAGEMENT AND KEEPING STRONG PERSONAL TIES WITH OUR COMMUNITY IS EXTREMELY IMPORTANT.

Encouraging Interaction

Now it's time to look at ways to encourage more of the engagements that spawn valuable conversations and relationships on Instagram. Likes, comments and mentions signal to Instagram that your content is high quality and that your account is relevant to certain people in your audience, so this type of interaction is clearly valuable in building your presence and community. This section includes tactics you can employ that will increase the amount of this kind of activity.

Your Instagram account should be the guy or girl that everyone wants to talk to at a party. At this party, it's in your best interest to speak to as many people as possible that might be interested in you. Your body language should signal that you're open to a conversation, you should smile at people and look approachable.

Instagram is the biggest open party on the Internet and you're probably already there, but who's coming to talk to you or telling you that they like your shoes?

The account to speak to

There are so many benefits to having an influential Instagram account, but unless your brand is already well known, you need to be clever about reaching that point.

Your account needs to be active, interactive and interesting. The more this comes across, the more people want to get involved. This can increase a kind of FOMO (fear of missing out) around your account, with people wanting to be the first to know about posts, competitions, polls and everything else.

The interactive elements of social media give fans the chance to be a part of your brand's journey and consciousness, even if it's just being one of hundreds of comments.

Engagement baiting

Simple tweaks to your posts and stories can inspire people to interact with your account. One of the simplest tactics is to employ some kind of call to action. These come in many forms, but are generally effective in encouraging the engagement promoted or requested by the call to action.

These engagements will signal relevancy in Instagram's algorithm, which, as we know, will help posts go further, contributing to the overall traction of the entire account. Some tried-and-tested tactics include the following:

- ◀ Putting a heart in the middle of a picture post emulates the heart that appears when someone double taps to like it.
- ◀ Creating 'Double tap if you agree' posts, where you directly encourage engagement as a response.
- ◀ Making typos or other errors in a post because people will reply to correct you. This is not recommended, and I don't advocate compromising your brand to generate engagement, but some crafty marketers swear by it!

Overcome your reservations

With brands opening up to their community, there can be a concern that people won't engage and you'll be left dancing on your own. Of course, requests for engagement that fall on deaf ears will have the opposite effect to the one you're seeking. However, there are many ways to invite engagement without looking like no one's listening.

One way is to ask questions in your Instagram stories. The responses are not public, so no one will know how many people replied. Another is to seed some people in your network who will comment on whatever you post. These could include brand ambassadors who commit to being the first people to comment. You might only need to do this for a short period; after that the community will respond unprompted.

The following seven rules will open the door for networks to engage with you; make it easy for people to respond to your content and start conversations; and introduce effective ways to attract engagements.

1. When following new accounts, like their posts

When you follow a new account, click through to their profile and like some of their posts.

IT HELPS YOU STAND OUT
Not only will they have a notification that you followed them, they will also have a separate notification for each of the posts that you liked. This means you take up more space on their notifications screen and they can see you have actually looked at their account before following them, making reciprocation more likely. You don't have to go to town on liking their posts; just the last one or two is perfect.

IT GENERATES ENGAGEMENT
The more feeds you appear on as soon as you post . . . the sooner you will receive likes . . . the more Instagram receives signals that you're posting good content . . . the more people your content is shown to . . . It's a snowball effect. You can artificially grow this snowball by engaging with others first.

IT GETS THE RELATIONSHIP OFF TO A GREAT START
Who knows? In the future this person might be a customer, or even a close friend. Create the best chance of a fruitful relationship by beginning it well. Don't be too proud to make the first move.

2. Invite responses to your stories

Generate story engagement by including text that specifically invites responses. Look for great excuses to start a conversation. People buy all sorts of weird and wonderful things for their house to act as conversation starters, to start the ball rolling in finding common ground with guests to their home. Turning your Instagram story into a conversation starter means more DM relationships, which has various benefits, including closer bonds with your followers.

Use your story text as you would your Instagram post captions, only be braver and bolder because people respond privately so no one will know how many responses you have received. It's the perfect opportunity to test out questions and monitor the response rate.

Use question captions to provide context to an image and resonate with people, inviting responses at the same time. You can get as creative as you like, but here are some examples to start with.

A place: Have you been here?

A new product: Would you buy this?

An old product: Do you have this?

An outfit: Do you think this suits me?!

A food item: Have you tried these?

A book: Have you read this?

TOP TIP The percentage response rate is the number of people who responded, divided by the number of people who viewed your story, multiplied by 100. Test out which types of questions command the most responses.

3. Ask for ideas and suggestions

The people who follow you represent valuable members of your target audience because they have already taken action in choosing to follow you. Their opinions can make the difference between creating products and providing services that sell well or don't sell at all.

When asking for ideas, opinions and suggestions, your questions must come from a place of confidence. You're not asking for assistance on fundamental aspects of your business; you're asking for insights that allow you to listen to your audience and build on a solid foundation.

PRODUCT VARIATIONS
If you're launching a product that will be available in multiple colours or styles, ask your audience which are their favourites.

CREATIVE DECISIONS
My children's storybook brand Clever Tykes asked their Instagram audience to help them decide on the outfit the main character wore in their next book.

CONTENT THEY'D LIKE TO SEE
Ask your audience what they'd like to see more of. This could be webinar topics, podcast themes, guests or more information about aspects of your business.

BUSINESS DECISIONS
If you're about to announce some news, see if your audience can guess what it is. That way you can respond to those who guess correctly or give clues to those who don't. If you're opening a new location, you could ask 'Where would you like our next location to be?' as part of the launch.

PROBLEM-SOLVING
If you're running a business, you exist to solve the problems of your customers and make their lives easier. Hearing about their obstacles and journeys better places you to do that.

Test these questions in your Instagram stories, then move some to captions once you're confident in the response rate.

4. Run an 'ask me anything' story

A great feature of Instagram stories is 'ask me anything' (AMA). This allows you to post an image or a video and add an AMA story sticker. This Instagram story then appears on your profile for 24 hours and questions are grouped together ready for you to answer and post responses to.

AMAs let you share more of your journey and shape your stories towards what your audience wants to see. They also provide opportunities for humour and enable your audience to get to know you better.

You can either run the AMA straight away, as the questions arrive, or you can run the AMA request over a 24-hour period, then answer all the questions at once.

When you see a question, click to respond and post the question along with your answer. Your response could be a video, a caption or a picture, and you can post more than one response to the same question. You don't have to answer every question and you don't have to disclose who asked the question, either. There's a lot of flexibility to have a lot of fun.

TOP TIPS

- Signpost beforehand when you'll be running your AMA, to ensure your audience prepares their questions.

- Signpost beforehand when you'll be answering the questions, so they know when to expect a response.

- Signal which topics you will be answering questions on. This is a great way of self-promoting, too!

Nervous you won't receive any questions? Don't leave it to chance. Tell a close friend which five questions you'd like them to ask, and get them to send them through. Planting specific questions sets the tone for the entire AMA and ensures you share the key messages.

5. Make use of Instagram story engagement features

Instagram stories allow you to add stickers over the top of your images or videos. The following four are the most engaging.

1. POLL
Lets you ask a question and then edit the default YES and NO to answers of your choosing. There is no right answer and the percentage of each response is displayed after an audience member clicks one.

2. QUIZ
Lets you pose a question and then give options. An audience member finds out the right answer after they click one. You can post multiple questions to keep people engaged for more than one story.

3. SLIDER
Lets someone move an emoji of a face with heart eyes up a slider, to share how much they love whatever is in the picture or video.

4. JOIN CHAT
Start a group chat on any topic you like, and use the story option to encourage people to join the chat. Name the chat and, as people click the button, you can choose who you let in to the chat.

The purpose of all of these examples is to generate engagement. Ask questions about your products, your brand, or just have some fun! The more interaction your story gets, the higher up the story order it will appear on the Instagram home page of your followers.

Keep your Instagram stories on-brand in their tone of voice, use of imagery, fonts and colours. They should be consistent with the look of your Instagram feed and offline presence.

6. Add your latest posts to your story

At any time, you can go to any of the posts on your home feed, click the paper airplane message underneath and click 'Add Post To Your Story'. Tapping the image (or video) then displays different ways of formatting the post on your story screen.

Do this when . . .

- ✈ You've posted something really important and want to ensure it's seen by as many of your followers as possible. Sharing new posts to your story means your content might appear on someone's home screen when they're scrolling across stories or scrolling down their feed.

- ✈ You want to encourage private engagement. Copy and paste the caption into your story as a text overlay to reiterate a question or request and give your followers an alternative way to respond.

- ✈ You want to boost profile visits or engagement on a particular post. If so, add text that encourages your audience to visit your profile to view your new post. Add a 'new post' sticker to catch their attention.

- ✈ You want to increase visibility on a specific Instagram location. If you've tagged the location in your post, tagging the location in the story too means you could feature twice on that location.

This trick became popular when people suspected the Instagram algorithm had changed, and they reported posts receiving lower engagements than usual. True or not, the more chance someone has of seeing your posts, the better the engagement rate they are likely to receive.

7. Run competitions

Running competitions can boost your account's engagement. It can spike your post comments and likes and allow you to begin relationships with a new set of users.

WHEN IS THIS USEFUL?
- ◅ To start a series of posts about one topic.
- ◅ To turn self-promotional information into an engaging content piece.
- ◅ To enhance the specific metric you're looking to improve.
- ◅ If you've been away from Instagram for a short period of time and you want to make a comeback.

Before running your competition, which could be via Instagram stories, a post, or from the link in your bio, be clear on the following elements.

- ◅ **The prize.** It should be big enough to attract attention but not so big that it seems unrealistic that someone might win it. Multiple prizes often work well in attracting entrants.
- ◅ **Entry requirements.** Be clear about what someone is required to do for their entry to be counted and make it straightforward.
- ◅ **Closing date.** Run competitions over a 24–72-hour period, but don't forget Instagram stories only last for 24 hours.
- ◅ **The date the winner(s) will be drawn.** Clearly communicate when the winners will be decided and how they will be notified.
- ◅ **How the winner(s) will be selected.** At random, or will there be a judge?

Ask your audience to do a maximum of two of the following in order to enter:

- ◀ like or comment on a specific post
- ◀ DM you
- ◀ swipe up to visit a page (if 10k+ followers)
- ◀ redirect to a specific contest page or another social media site
- ◀ user-generated, require people to tag you in story (and share)
- ◀ respond to questions
- ◀ complete a quiz
- ◀ follow you.

Once you've run one competition, assess the response and plan your next one. The best and most engaging Instagram accounts run competitions at regular intervals and their followers look forward to them.

Chapter Four
Growth

The world of social media never stands still, so neither must you. If your account remains static, the brands around you will overtake and you're at risk of becoming irrelevant. The growth of your Instagram account demonstrates that you're hitting the right notes when it comes to content and that your brand is reaching and appealing to more and more individuals.

What growth means

Growing your Instagram account could refer to several different things, but in this chapter we're specifically talking about increasing your influence on the platform. Instagram account owners often strive to increase their brand's reach, engagement rates and the number of followers. And while all of these are noble goals in their own right, they will also contribute towards larger pursuits, building awareness of your brand and ensuring more people reach your website from Instagram, for example.

So while these smaller goals might seem like vanity metrics on the surface, they're the perfect means via which to measure 'growth'.

Remember that every Instagram account starts with zero followers. The growth in followers is therefore what differentiates more successful brand accounts from those that aren't quite there yet. Of course, there are many factors at play when it comes to accruing followers, including how well known an individual or brand already is, especially when it comes to the initial spike in an account's following. While you may not have this privilege, plenty of others like you have managed to grow their accounts rapidly, so you can too.

Why growth is paramount

There are countless benefits that come with growing your account. Your content goes further, you receive more engagements and it opens doors for you. New opportunities arise as you become a bigger player in your niche; you have more sway and you're in greater demand from audience members, other brands and media outlets.

Sheer weight of numbers counts too. Some people interpret follower-count as an authority signal so they might instantly have an impression of you as a well-liked and trusted brand. People like to associate themselves with success. If enough people proudly follow your account, even without chance of you following them in return, it conveys a certain level of status. Capitalise on these mechanisms and keep your account growing.

Maximise your influence

Follower-count underpins the influence you have on Instagram. It is the 'quantity' in the 'quality vs quantity' equation. Whatever you're selling or promoting, the more followers you have, the more people you reach and the faster word gets out. If enough people proudly follow your account, especially without you following them in return, it conveys a certain level of status as a well-liked and trusted brand.

This will serve you very well, whatever your needs, as people like to associate themselves with success. The products you launch will sell faster. Events will sell out. Customer feedback will happen instantly. Public opinion will be swayed. Through account growth, you become the influencer.

The ultimate goal

Growth is probably the hardest element of the Instagram game to crack because you have little direct control over it. Profile optimisation, creating great content and engaging with your audience can all be done on a daily basis, but results will vary.

The good news is that social-media growth can be exponential. Every like and comment you receive will increase the number of people that post reaches. Every new follower you attract is a chance to reach more members of your audience. With the right recipe for growth, you can apply the same efforts with increasingly better results.

The four steps to achieving growth

This chapter is split into the following four areas:

1. Gaining Traction
2. Reaching New Audiences
3. Paid Advertising
4. Measuring Results

Gaining Traction

Traction is a fundamental concept in social media marketing, at both the individual post and entire account level. Learning how to maximise traction will make your account grow faster.

Reaching New Audiences

In order to grow, you have to find a way to regularly reach new audiences. If you always follow the same content and interaction strategies, your audience growth is likely to be slow. Unlocking groups of new audience members can rapidly generate an influx of new followers.

Paid Advertising

With the right targeting and content, paid ads will help grow your Instagram account. By making small iterations to increase their effectiveness, they can represent excellent value and a great source of new followers and reach.

Measuring Results

By keeping a close eye on which of your endeavours results in the fastest rate of growth or the best value growth, you can better focus your efforts. Measuring results and adapting your strategy accordingly is the difference between haphazard growth and consistent, scalable growth.

Gaining Traction

Traction is essentially the rise in reach and influence that a post or account generates at any given time. Without traction, momentum is incredibly difficult to generate and it feels like you're treading water. You might be keeping your head above water but you're spending a lot of energy staying put.

Traction is most important at the start – both of building an Instagram account and building a business. Without traction it's easy to give up, as doubts creep in about the validity of your ideas and whether success will ever be possible.

Traction occurs at both the post and account level. The mechanisms, timescales and impacts involved at these two levels are very different.

Post-level traction

The traction that a single post gains is largely down to Instagram's algorithm. Positive engagement signals that the post is increasingly relevant to a wider audience and so the post is shown to more people. Further reach and engagements proliferate this effect and traction is in full flow.

This is how posts go viral on social media. In the main, however, while posts can generate huge levels of reach, they usually only have a temporary impact; a transient spike in post metrics. This is the case unless a post happens to be so compelling that it results in a significant number of new followers or even sales.

Account-level traction

At an account level, we're more concerned with long-term growth in account size and influence – week to week, month to month, and even year to year. There are many metrics we can look at to determine the traction of an account, as well as the rate of change in these metrics over time.

What it looks like when you have traction

At both post and account level, there is a snowball effect as they gather momentum quickly. Posts reach more people, more people engage and comment, and yet more people begin to tag, mention and share your content or brand name. This assists in reaching even more people who decide to follow and do the same.

Cristiano Ronaldo's Instagram account is a great example of traction. The account is at 229 million followers, but on an average day in the last week, his account grew by 189,000 followers, regardless of whether he actually posted anything. He's definitely at one extreme of the scale, but you can see how popular and well-loved accounts amass more followers. On a smaller but still impressive scale, athlete Dr Stefi Cohen has 845,000 followers and her account grows by around 200–1,000 followers per day.

Reasons brands don't build traction

There are several reasons a brand on Instagram might not be able to generate traction, and if you find yourself in this situation it is crucial to work out which of the following is most likely.

- Your content isn't compelling enough.
- There's no demand for your product or services.
- Your audience needs educating first.
- Your messaging is not resonating.
- There are too many competitors in the market.

Some of these issues may be insurmountable and there may be a fundamental flaw in your business that even the most cunning of marketing campaigns can't solve. However, others are the result of shortcomings in your marketing strategy which, given enough time and resource commitment, will be overcome.

It may be a single post or even a hashtag that gives you the traction you need to gain an initial spike in followers and a much-needed boost of confidence.

1. Leverage the algorithm

Instagram's primary goal is to maximise the time users spend on the platform because the longer users linger, the more ads they see. So directly or indirectly, accounts that help Instagram achieve that goal are rewarded.

The Instagram algorithm is complex and ever-evolving. It will dictate how far a post reaches and the traction it achieves and has the power to make posts go viral.

Instagram doesn't disclose much about the algorithm and how it works. They give some things away on their own social media sites, at conferences and in press releases; insights are gleaned and hypotheses tested, but users can never fully know because it would be too easy to gamify if confirmed.

INSTAGRAM'S TOP THREE RANKING SIGNALS

1. Relationship
Instagram prioritises the posts and stories from the people you interact with the most. So the more you DM someone, tag them in your content or just generally engage with them, the more Instagram will think their content is relevant for you to see and vice versa. So the closer you are with your network – the more engaged and in contact – the more prominent your content will be on their Instagram feed.

2. Interest
Instagram estimates people's appetite for your content based on past trends. An individual's online presence will have a history of their likes and interests, all of which tell a story of who they are. The more relevant your content to your followers' interests and the more consistent you are with it, the more likely it is to feature prominently in their feeds.

3. Timeliness
Although Instagram is no longer in chronological order, it does prioritise newer posts. This means that posting when your audience is online is key to hitting the timeliness algorithm rank.

2. Keep your quality consistently high

In the game of Instagram traction, effort has a compound effect. Making sure your Instagram account is properly set up and looks great, creating post after post, diligently doing your outreach, analysing, learning and editing, might seem like a chore, but it will be worth it.

Ramping up your input for one month will result in higher engagement levels and growth of your account, providing the content is good quality and directly relevant to your audience. Keeping this effort consistent in month two will mean the growth happens again, but this time by more. Each month your numbers go up by more than they did in the previous month, and so it keeps going.

Consistency has been a key factor through much of this book, but growth is where consistency of brand, content, engagement and timing come together to turn your account into a sizeable force.

Set yourself new challenges to keep up momentum and motivation. Capitalise on a popular post by posting again and riding the wave. Make sure your content is high in quality, so it is always seen favourably. Use the results of each post to set the bar higher, then post again. Make it your mission that every month the consistency and quality is there across every input.

3. Evolve your account as necessary

Throughout your Instagram journey there will be key milestones: opening your account or posting for the first time; sending your first story; winning your first follower.

After that, it's having more followers than the number of accounts you are following. Then it's your posts consistently reaching 100 likes, then 1,000, then 10,000. Soon there are follower milestones, including hitting 10,000 followers and being able to use the 'swipe up' function. Perhaps you have dreams of being a verified account.

Throughout this evolution, ensure every part of your account steps up. When you're a bigger brand, you need to act like a bigger brand. Freshen it up and aim to appeal to new audiences, or reflect the changes in your existing audience, to prevent stagnation. Don't let your audience get bored of your content and keep coming up with ideas and inspiration to make sure that doesn't happen.

HOW TO EVOLVE YOUR INSTAGRAM

Content: Get better at taking photos, improve the quality of your kit, or hire a professional. Learn new techniques and let fewer posts through that you're not 100 per cent happy with.

Stories: Design your stories before posting them, add subtitles to videos, move towards how a large, image-conscious brand would use stories.

Bio and links: Revisit them at every milestone and check they still reflect the brand you want to be, not the brand that you have outgrown.

TOP TIP When your brand has evolved to be a pretty big deal, encourage your audience to 'turn on notifications' for your posts. If you're confident that enough people will do it, it's a nice way to stay ahead of the algorithm, and even making the request signals a level of assurance.

4. Secure more traditional PR coverage

Many Instagram accounts with large followings didn't grow their accounts purely through Instagram. The people and brands behind these accounts achieved success, fame or recognition in the real world or through a different media.

This explains why an existing celebrity can open an account and instantly amass thousands of followers. They already have a huge fan base, so they can ignore all the rules and still see incredible traction. Many celebrity accounts are inconsistent, share badly made videos and images, never use hashtags and post sporadically, yet still their accounts grow.

Instagram accounts with the most substance are those that would quickly regain all of their followers if their account was to be closed and reopened from scratch. If someone actively searches for your account instead of passively scrolling and coming across your content on their home feed, you are becoming invaluable to your audience.

Developing your reputation within your industry, becoming known as a key person of influence, being invited for interviews and features, winning awards and being known as an expert in your field will mean people are interested by you and look to follow you online. Increasing the profile of yourself or your brand and putting yourself in the limelight, attracts attention, which translates to Instagram followers.

On the other hand, simply using Instagram well can mean that your account is publicised simply because it's using Instagram well. Every year there are awards ceremonies that celebrate 'Best use of social media' finalists. A quick google of those taking place near you could give you a good opportunity to draw attention to what you're doing and reap the rewards of the publicity.

5. Get references and links to your profile

Website search-engine optimisation (SEO) involves building links to a website to help Google see it as authoritative. Now think of this as Instagram SEO. The more places that link to your account, the more likely you are to be found by people outside Instagram. Include your username in everything you do to help more people find you.

EVENTS
If you sponsor, speak at or even just attend events, include your username on any printed material you distribute, or on any slides you use when presenting. If an event has a live Instagram board, get involved.

ONLINE LISTS
Look for existing 'best of' lists and reach out to the author. A sushi restaurant searching 'Best Instagram accounts about sushi' can reach out to the top 10 of the 145 million results for that phrase to ask the people compiling those lists if they want to include their account.

YOUR WRITING
If you submit press releases to secure news articles about your company, include your username. If you carry out any guest blogging, find a way of linking to your own content.

ARTICLES AND NEWS STORIES
Subscribe to journalistic tool 'Help A Reporter Out' (HARO) to respond to journalists looking for sources and ask that if your answers are used in their piece that they include a link to your Instagram account.

6. Read relevant case studies

Interviewing the contributors for the case studies included in this book was fascinating. While everyone's journey was different, each account was intentional about growing their Instagram network and hungry for tips and new ideas.

The same tactics won't work for every account or every audience or every time period. However, at any given time there will be accounts employing tactics that are just enough ahead of the curve to stand out and gain traction.

Focus your research
This goes beyond researching the latest Instagram features; this is the application of the latest Instagram features.

Instagram tools
Hopper and Later consistently write blogs to explore the best ways of using Instagram updates. Social media tools and agencies such as Flaunt Report and JC Social Media publish articles on tried-and-tested tactics, using specific examples.

Lists
Lists of 'best [type of business] on Instagram' pop up all the time, giving insights into how businesses like yours have grown their accounts. You can also search '[type of business] Instagram case study' for specific examples.

What's attracted your attention?
Think about the latest accounts you followed. Why did you decide to follow them? Did they do anything differently that you can look to emulate in your own actions?

Online experts on Instagram
Individuals who rely on Instagram to create income are using it well and are likely exploring all sorts of ways to stand out. Some of the most successful Instagram methods I've used for my clients have come from friends whose businesses rely on them making a connection with their audience online.

7. Make a schedule for following accounts

The simplest way to grow your following is to follow more accounts. A follow-back culture exists on Instagram, so this method can be incredibly powerful, especially when starting an account from scratch. Following accounts that represent relevant members of your target audience is likely to mean they follow you back.

Efficient Instagram processes require the batching of actions, and following accounts is no different. Batch your efforts into follow sprees two or three times per week and switch up which time of day you are active. Make a schedule to stick to involving how many you follow each time you carry out a spree. Start small then ramp up.

Throughout this process, keep an eye on your own follower numbers and ratios. Follow enough accounts so that you look engaged, but not so many that the ratio isn't right. Done in the right way, following accounts suits most brands.

TOP TIP If an account's follower:following ratio is close to 1:1, they're more likely to follow you back. Accounts that have far more followers than they follow are less likely to follow back.

LET'S TALK ABOUT BOTS
Accounts that use automated programs (bots) to carry out this process for them can grow their accounts quickly. Bots exist but they are against Instagram guidelines; Instagram wants real people carrying out natural human behaviour rather than gaming the platform. Real people will click on ads, which is how Instagram is monetised.

Instagram has limits on the number of accounts you can follow and unfollow per day, even if you're doing it manually. This is to avoid this method being spammy or of detriment to other users.

8. Use an app for unfollowing and cleaning your account

When you click on the profile of someone you follow on Instagram, it's not immediately clear whether they follow you back. To find out, you need to click on who they follow and search for your username.

Regularly clearing the list of who you follow will keep your following number low, your ratio under control and free up space to follow new people. Using apps is the simplest and quickest way to clear your following list of people who don't follow you back. FindUnfollow and Instacleaner allow you to add your Instagram account and select all non-followers. You can then select to unfollow them from the app, being mindful of Instagram's unfollow limits.

RUN A SCHEDULE
Monday: Follow 100 accounts

Thursday: Unfollow people who don't follow you back and follow 100 more accounts

Monday: Repeat . . .

This should spike interest and growth alongside your strong content and interaction game.

If having more followers than following is important to you, when you hit a specific follower number, revisit your entire following list and consider unfollowing accounts, even if they follow you.

WHAT IF SOMEONE UNFOLLOWS ME?
Accounts lose followers all the time, so don't see it as a big deal when it happens to you. Someone might have closed their account, been suspended by Instagram, used a follow app themselves, had a thorough clearout, or perhaps your account no longer represents their interests. In all cases, it's no problem. Don't dwell on who unfollowed you because it really doesn't matter.

Reaching New Audiences

The ability of your brand to reach new audiences is a fundamental component of growth. There are many different mechanisms via which this can be achieved, whether through your content and interaction on Instagram, or outside the platform entirely.

Your core audience and community can generally be reached through more traditional growth tactics, so this section looks at techniques specifically designed to tap into audiences who have been oblivious to your existence or who you've so far been unable to enchant.

New followers can come from anywhere

Be open-minded about where new followers can be discovered. It's time to focus on the people that you've not been able to reach with your primary content and engagement strategies. This may require some creative thinking and proactivity in getting your account or even just your username in front of fresh eyes.

Remember that Instagram remains a growing social network, so potential new followers are arriving on a daily basis. This means that there are opportunities both online and in the real world to happen upon someone who has an Instagram account and would like to keep up to date with you and your brand.

Every follower counts

Don't underestimate the value of any single follower. Your content is likely to show prominently to new followers and the engagement you secure from them may in turn put your content in front of some of their network. A single follower might not seem significant, but gaining one with 20,000 followers of their own gives your account more clout and opens up a lot of potential.

There's also the chance that any new follower will one day become a customer or superfan with a very real and significant benefit. Sometimes it's impossible to predict how the relationship with a new follower will evolve, so never discount anyone or pass up an opportunity to expand your network.

New followers evolve your brand

Meeting people, building your network, selling products and providing services are all examples of interactions that can translate to Instagram followers and open new relationships. Every time you uncover a previously untapped source of followers, your brand changes. The community it serves will be different, if only slightly. It's likely you'll learn something about your brand and your audience; it may turn out that your brand or product is super relevant to a sub-niche you didn't even know existed. This could open up new content and hashtag ideas and may influence how you portray your brand.

Each of the following seven rules has the potential to unlock a pocket of fresh followers. They cover a wide range of ideas to bear in mind and test and any one of them could be the catalyst for finding new followers and enabling new growth, which starts the snowball effect.

1. Collaborate with users to cross-promote

Leverage accounts with large networks to reach your audience and gain invaluable third-party endorsement. Micro-influencers are roughly defined as having between 5,000 and 50,000 followers. Many of them will promote a product they are gifted (providing they like it) and some will set fees for sponsored posts, stories or product placement.

HOW TO IDENTIFY COLLABORATORS

1. **Shared audience.** Do some research on their audience and check how much crossover it has with your target demographics.

2. **Shared ethos.** Ensure their brand values align with yours for consistency in messaging and framing.

3. **Things in common.** Ensure your account has enough in common with theirs in order for a collaboration to make sense to both of your audiences.

After shortlisting a handful of micro-influencers to approach, message them. Ask for their rates and explain your offer and what you'd like in return. Remember: micro-influencers are real people, who might be sceptical about introducing new brands to their audience. Aim to understand them and work out a plan that is mutually beneficial.

BEFORE SIGNING A DEAL

- Ask to see case studies of brands they've worked with, including metrics of successful campaigns and testimonials from clients.

- Look at their engagement rates on posts as a percentage of their total follower number. Assess whether their audience seems engaged and trusting of them.

- Check for falsified engagement. Sometimes blogger circles carry out engagement on each other's content to falsify engagement numbers.

- ◀ Batch your deals. Results can vary between accounts, so run collaborator campaigns in clusters.
- ◀ Check there's no conflict of interest. Do they promote competing products to yours?

Set your terms

- ◀ Be clear what you would like to see in return for the fee or product and come to a reasonable agreement that is documented in writing.
- ◀ Include the preferred way of presenting or using your products and some dos and don'ts to ensure your brand is portrayed in the best light.

One way of maintaining more control over a collaboration is to host the micro-influencers: organise a shoot, look after them, cover their expenses and hire a photographer or videographer. Create content and share the image files with them so they can post them too.

TOP TIP Use the website BloggersRequired to post assignments and have people apply to promote your product. You can list paid assignments or the reward could be the product itself.

2. Network in new groups

Charlie 'Tremendous' Jones once said, 'Five years from today you will be the same person that you are today, except for the people you meet and the books that you read.'

The more people you know, the more people will find you online. Expanding your network will translate into growth of your Instagram, but you will need to actively create the link for this to happen. This strategy involves ramping up how sociable you are. Look for new groups to be a part of and mingle within.

ONLINE NETWORKS
Find networks that connect like-minded people and join some new tribes. There are networks, groups and associations out there for every profession and hobby you can imagine. Explore every interest or skill you have and use it to meet more people with that in common.

FACEBOOK GROUPS
Each online network will have an accompanying Facebook group where you can meet people at all stages of their journey. Facebook groups often have set days of the week where members can share their business or a challenge they are facing, to gain support from the group. Some groups have specific comment threads designed to share Instagram handles. Get involved.

MEETING PEOPLE IN REAL LIFE
Sign up to events, go to more parties or gatherings, or just make an effort to chat to more people in your current day-to-day life. Make it your mission to meet new people and cultivate new relationships. Get to know people, find out their stories. Be a sociable person and, when the time is right, talk about Instagram too. Don't assume someone will find you.

3. Use your other social networks

Connect your other social media accounts to your Instagram. Sharing your handle or nametag on your other social network profiles is a quick and simple way of moving followers over to Instagram. Instagram itself has some options for how you do this, including linking your Facebook profile, your address book contacts and other social networks including Twitter and Tumblr.

If Instagram is the only feed you regularly populate, set it to auto-post across other platforms. That way you'll keep reminding your Facebook, Twitter and Tumblr connections of your Instagram.

If you update Twitter, LinkedIn or Facebook regularly, refer your audience on each platform to your Instagram account. Send out teasers. Share one image on Twitter, for example, and signpost that the rest of the collection is on your Instagram.

To avoid any confusion, make it clear what people will find on your Instagram account when you link to it from other platforms. If you use Twitter for your law firm day job and Instagram for your gaming blogger side hustle, say so. Don't leave anyone surprised.

TOP TIP Send an update asking your Twitter followers, LinkedIn connections and Facebook friends to tell you their Instagram handles, then follow them first.

4. Create your nametag

Your Instagram nametag can be created and designed via your Instagram app. It allows someone to find you on Instagram by scanning your nametag rather than typing your username.

Create your nametag by clicking 'nametag' in Instagram's options. Touch anywhere on the screen to customise it. Use 'colour' to switch between different colours, 'emoji' to choose an emoji design, or 'selfie' to take a photo and try on different selfie stickers.

You can scan nametags from your Instagram story screen by pointing your camera at the nametag and pressing and holding your screen. Instagram then finds the accompanying profile to allow you to follow and interact.

You can share your nametag across your other social networks and Instagram also gives you the option to save your nametag as an image so you can print it on merchandise or stickers. Add it to your website or email signature for a colourful way of attracting attention. At some conferences, attendees' lanyards display their nametag, to easily connect with other guests online after meeting at the event.

Take your nametag further by displaying it at your premises. Think creatively about incorporating it into your events, exhibitor stands, flyers, brochures or even on cupcakes!

5. Make your Instagram handle visible

Make it easy for people to find you by adding your Instagram handle to multiple places within your business.

YOUR WEBSITE
Your website should have a prominent link to your brand's Instagram page. Use the latest version of Instagram's logo, and look into displaying your feed posts or providing a strong call-to-action. Include a link on your contact page, too.

YOUR PROFILE PAGE ON YOUR COMPANY
If you're part of an organisation that uses team member profile pages, use this opportunity to link to your Instagram.

PRODUCTS
Every product you use now has an Instagram handle printed on it: food packaging, product boxes, even toothpaste tubes display that familiar @ sign. If your brand creates products of any kind, look for opportunities to include yours.

YOUR PLACE OF WORK
If you serve customers from a fixed location, display your handle somewhere they will see it. Areas where people are likely to be waiting around are perfect: the wall by the bathroom queue, a waiting room, or behind a bar.

WEAR YOUR HANDLE
Search 'Instagram handle' in Etsy and find multiple results for personalised items you can buy, from clothing to bumper stickers to handmade jewellery and doggy accessories. If that's your vibe, have your handle printed on everything!

OTHER PROFILES
You can link to your Instagram on Goodreads, Medium, your Amazon author page, industry-specific websites or listings, including TripAdvisor or Google My Business – basically anywhere you have an online profile. A surprising number of people use Tinder as a way to grow their Instagram following; setting up your profile includes the option to add your Instagram handle, and some users employing this tactic noticed as many as 100 new followers per day.

6. See everyone as a collaborator, not a competitor

Instagram growth is not a zero sum game. There are enough followers, engagement and opportunities to go around.

Don't see anyone as a competitor. Your crossover areas with another account are unlikely to be exactly the same, which means there's always an opportunity to learn and grow.

Consider:

- ◀ Two interior design firms on Instagram, each serving a different niche of clients.

- ◀ Two networks for female entrepreneurs on Instagram, each offering different products to help their members.

- ◀ Two speciality coffee shops on Instagram, each operating within a different geographic area.

Each of these pairs might think they are competitors, but they have more in common than they think. Communicating with each other and sharing ideas will benefit both accounts.

Even if you think that something has been done before, chances are not everyone will have seen it before. Your own take on anything is original, even if it's been inspired by a different account.

If a 'competitor' follows you, be flattered! If they want to take inspiration from you, let them. Don't worry about someone else's game, focus on yours. Collaboration always beats competitiveness, so don't close off avenues and pockets of potential new followers by imagining a problem that isn't there.

7. Push the boundaries

Instagram has rules known as 'community guidelines' and 'terms of use'. These include respecting others, only posting material you have the right to share, abiding by the law and fostering genuine interactions. Many of Instagram's no-nos include spammy methods of artificially collecting likes, followers or shares.

Some practices are strictly forbidden by Instagram and some are tolerated. Make sure you understand what falls within the guidelines and don't fall for scams promising quick wins that could compromise your account or get it suspended.

The following activities are not endorsed by me or this book, but you will likely become aware of them through your increased use of Instagram. Approach with caution.

INSTAGRAM PODS
These range from informal groups liking each other's content, to huge private networks which work to falsify engagement in order to boost reach. Instagram has worked to close Instagram pods set up as Facebook groups and develops its algorithm to detect people operating within them.

FOLLOW AND UNFOLLOW APPS
Automation is against Instagram's terms of use. Some apps update their software to get around Instagram's rules and mimic human behaviour so as not to be flagged, but it's a risky business. Some follow and unfollow apps are within Instagram's guidelines, but check before you sign up.

BUYING FOLLOWERS
Websites that sell followers will claim that it's safe, but don't risk it. Many of them will be bots or inactive accounts, so they won't engage with your posts. They're probably not within your target demographic, so Instagram won't know what your account stands for and it's against Instagram's policy.

Do your research before engaging in any activity on Instagram that could be against Instagram's guidelines; never give out your password and if in doubt, say no.

What The Fab, USA
@WTFAB

Elise Armitage, Digital content creator

The travel and fashion influencer making a living from her Instagram account.

Elise started her lifestyle and travel-focused blog in 2012 and her Instagram account in 2014. She left her job at Google at the beginning of 2019 to focus on them full time.

When she first started her Instagram account it was just for fun; she had no idea it would turn into something she could monetise. Now, 136,000 followers later, she has quarterly revenue goals that she is looking to hit with her Instagram collaborations.

TELL ME ABOUT THE PURPOSE OF YOUR ACCOUNT AND HOW IT FITS WITH YOUR LIFE.

Instagram is one of my main sources of income. I do sponsored brand collaborations where I shoot original content for brands, share them with my audience and talk about how the brand fits into my own lifestyle.

Since I quit my full-time job, my account has definitely become more business-focused. I'm looking at it both in terms of what would my audience enjoy and find helpful, but also, what would make a brand want to work with me?

WHAT DO YOU DO EACH WEEK?

I post five days a week and I try to do a balance of sponsored and non-sponsored content. I also spend time engaging with other accounts, as well as responding to comments and DMs on my own account.

I want my profile and photos to inspire people, but to also be relatable. I never want someone to feel envious or bad about themselves after looking at my account. Rather, I hope that my profile inspires them to plan their next trip, save for a new fashion item they've been lusting over, or apply a lifestyle tip I'm sharing to live their best lives.

HAS YOUR ACCOUNT GROWN FASTER AT CERTAIN POINTS AND, IF SO, WHY?

Absolutely; 2017 and 2018 were both years where my account steadily grew. It was much easier to grow your account then because simply by engaging with other accounts, you would drive eyeballs back to your own Instagram profile and people would follow you. Now, Instagram is saturated and it's much more difficult to grow. I make plans for my account's growth and I track my goals in a spreadsheet.

CAN YOU PREDICT HOW WELL A POST WILL DO BEFORE YOU POST IT?

Usually I can. Posts with me or my face in them tend to perform better than those without. People like human connection, but occasionally a post that I think might not perform as well will surprise me and get higher engagement than expected, including products, travel scenes or stylish interior shots of spaces I shoot from.

HOW MUCH HASHTAG RESEARCH DO YOU DO?

I spend about an hour per week on hashtag research. I'm usually looking for hashtags in my travel and lifestyle niche that have been used 50–250,000 times on other posts. Anything more than that makes it too difficult to land on that hashtag's top page.

DO YOU HAVE KNOWLEDGE OF INSTAGRAM'S ALGORITHM?

I know some general tips and rules for what the algorithm 'likes', based on talking with other influencers and my own experiences.

For example, I recently posted an Instagram story where I mentioned that I was sharing something really personal in my latest post and it resulted in a larger than normal amount of my audience tapping through to that post. For weeks after that story, my Instagram story views were much higher than usual.

I believe it was because the increase in my audience taking that action of tapping through to my photo signalled to the algorithm that my content was interesting, resulting in the algorithm boosting my stories for weeks afterward for more people to see.

HAVE YOU CREATED YOUR OWN RULES FOR YOUR BRAND AND YOUR ACCOUNT'S VOICE?

Whenever I'm writing my captions, I imagine I'm talking to my sister or a close girlfriend, and that helps me keep my writing in my own voice. For my photos, I keep them light, colourful and happy to fit my brand aesthetic.

I get a lot of inspiration for content from my travels, as well as my eclectic city, San Francisco.

DO YOU BOOST/PROMOTE CONTENT?

I've been experimenting with boosting content, especially when a brand I'm working with wants to put additional budget towards boosting. It means I can be more certain how far that post will reach, and who those people are.

I RECENTLY POSTED AN INSTAGRAM STORY WHERE I MENTIONED THAT I WAS SHARING SOMETHING REALLY PERSONAL IN MY LATEST POST, AND IT RESULTED IN A LARGER THAN NORMAL AMOUNT OF MY AUDIENCE TAPPING THROUGH TO THAT POST.

POSTS WITH ME OR MY FACE IN THEM TEND TO PERFORM BETTER THAN THOSE WITHOUT ME IN THEM, BUT OCCASIONALLY A POST THAT I THINK MIGHT NOT PERFORM AS WELL WILL SURPRISE ME

Paid Advertising

Since Facebook acquired Instagram in 2014, there has been a concerted effort to expand and improve the paid advertising element of the platform. Facebook has infamously restricted the organic reach of business pages on its own site, virtually forcing businesses to invest in advertising.

Instagram hasn't gone quite the same way yet, but there's still a lot of value in paid advertising. Paid ads pretty much guarantee a certain level of reach and engagement for a brand, whether it's well established or was founded yesterday.

Managing your Instagram ads

This section is going to look at the actual mechanics of setting up and running ads on Instagram, but to cover the absolute basics or for the full extent of the ads platform, I recommend Facebook's Blueprint.

In short, your ads will be split into campaigns with distinct goals. Each campaign will contain ad sets, which may focus on achieving these goals in slightly different ways: perhaps targeting a different audience, promoting a different deal or using different types of messaging. Within each ad set there are the individual ads, which will have different visual collateral, copy and calls to action.

When advertising on Instagram, always use Facebook Business Manager to set up your campaigns. This is best done from a desktop computer.

Instagram accounts are linked to their Facebook counterpart. This means that Facebook's ads platform utilises information collected over both in order to profile users. So despite Instagram appearing to collect less personal information than Facebook, you are still able to target adverts with a high degree of granularity.

Like Facebook, Instagram allows businesses the ability to target audiences on a range of factors: age, gender, demographics, interests, behaviour and activity.

This means you can fairly accurately put your content in front of the individuals you suspect are in your target audience. You don't rely on your content gaining traction and reaching new people who may or may not be in your audience; in a sense, you're paying Instagram to do that work for you.

But it's not quite as simple as spending money on a post and seeing the sales roll in. Ads must be set up and executed cleverly, and you'll need to analyse the data and make smart decisions.

Stats

One of the most useful elements of running paid ads is that you are provided with performance data. This enables you to judge the effectiveness of certain messaging or imagery and work to hone your strategy.

Value

Through accurate targeting, appealing content and the effective utilisation of the data your ads collect, you can achieve some valuable results. It's possible to secure metrics of a matter of pennies each, completely legitimately, although there are many factors that affect this.

It is possible to do one-off boosted posts, directly via Instagram, whereby a piece of content you have shared can be promoted to a targeted audience. While this will give these posts a 'boost', they shouldn't form part of your paid ads strategy. It is far more effective to run campaigns from Facebook's Business Manager and to tweak ads and audiences as you interpret statistics and your account evolves.

These contrasting approaches can be likened to putting coins in a slot machine versus buying shares. One is a quick, no-thought activity; the other is a long-term investment involving planning and research. Pick the latter.

1. Try different types of ad campaign

Advertising on Instagram is a journey of trial and error. Even if you read countless case studies, you won't know for sure what will work for your brand until you try things out, learn and continue to adapt.

Instagram users engage in different ways with different ads. Each ad you post will display the word 'Sponsored' above it. It's paramount that your ad resonates with someone very quickly because often users will click away as soon as they realise they are being advertised to. Instagram is a personal place, so create ads that favour lifestyle over product or catalogue shots.

Begin by trying different types of ad campaign.

SINGLE IMAGE ADS
Set up an ad and use one strong image as the only media. Add your caption underneath. For best results, use an image that originally performed well organically.

VIDEO ADS
Set up an ad and use a video as the only media. Before posting, check the videos's duration, ensure the intro gets straight into the action, and check it works with the sound turned off, or add captions or subtitles. Within Ads Manager, you can also choose the cover for your video, which is the frame that displays on the explore tab or home feed before the video starts to play.

Your video could also consist of multiple images transitioning or cutting onto the screen. Create this separately and upload to the platform.

CAROUSEL

Set up an ad as a 'carousel' to include multiple (minimum 2, maximum 10) images. Users can then choose to flip through them. For best results, use square images and put your strongest one first.

For each of the above ad types you can choose to optimise for reach and engagement or clickthroughs. If you want to direct people to an external page, add a link. If you don't, ensure the caption is written to encourage responses.

STORY ADS

Story ads display when users scroll through their Instagram stories. Format your images or videos in portrait mode and focus on high-quality images and a composition that will grab attention straight away, to keep someone watching.

TOP TIP The best ads look like the type of content your audience's friends would post. The more someone believes your content is organic and that they have chosen to see it, even if for a short space of time, the better it is likely to perform when promoted. Keep this in mind when designing your ads.

2. Target your audience

Take the core audience you defined in Chapter One and translate this to the audience you will advertise to.

- ◂ **Age:** choose a lower and an upper audience age range.
- ◂ **Location:** choose specific towns, cities or countries, or pinpoint a place and define a radius around it. Add as many areas as you like; you can also add exclusions.
- ◂ **Gender:** if your products and services are for all genders, ignore this field. If they are for specific genders, then narrow it down.
- ◂ **Language:** if you include text anywhere in your ad or captions, ensure the language field is correct to make sure they're shown to the right audience.
- ◂ **Connections:** this allows you to narrow by how people are connected to your pages, apps or events – for example, to exclude those who already like your page.

DETAILED TARGETING
This is where it gets really interesting. Detailed targeting is focused on three sections: demographics, interests and behaviours. Use the 'Browse' option to move between them.

- ◂ Demographics is split by education, financial, life events, parents, relationship and work. Use this section to create a picture of your perfect audience member.
- ◂ Interests are grouped into nine categories, including hobbies & activities and entertainment. Refine your audience further by selecting from these lists, then click 'Suggestions' to see how the Ads Manager suggests you improve your targeting.
- ◂ Behaviours includes options for over 10 areas, including purchase behaviour, how much someone travels for work or pleasure and even which internet browser they use. Use this to go into detail on how your target audience acts – for example, if they have a long commute, if they travel often, the mobile device they use and how much they use it.

ADVANCED TARGETING

- ◄ **Custom audiences:** this is where you can instal Facebook's pixel to your site and advertise to people who take certain actions on your website. You could also upload a database and advertise to these people across Instagram.
- ◄ **Lookalike:** this is where the ads platform finds other users who are similar to those you have specified, allowing you to expand your targeting.

Check the gauge on the right-hand side to see Facebook's recommendations for how narrow your audience is. Too narrow and your ads won't be shown; too wide and your ads won't resonate as tightly. Think harder about narrowing your audience down and make use of AND/OR criteria.

For example, showing ads to an audience that likes gardening AND insects will be narrower and more specific than an audience that likes gardening OR insects. The former audience will likely contain more appropriate individuals.

NEXT STEPS

1. Set up your core audience in Facebook's Ads Manager, selecting 'Audiences' from the ads menu.
2. Go through the same process to set up a secondary audience, consisting of people in a slightly different demographic.
3. Run the same ads to each audience and see which performs the best.
4. Take the best performing audience and create a Lookalike Audience from it. Run the same ads to this audience, too.

3. Set up your ads monitoring dashboard

Once you're familiar with Ads Manager, you'll be able to easily assess results and progress your campaigns. Do this by setting up a dashboard that displays all the information you need at a glance.

HOW TO SET UP YOUR DASHBOARD

- Log in to Ads Manager and click on 'Campaigns' to see all your campaigns at a high level. This is the start of your dashboard.
- Use 'Columns' and 'Customise columns' to drag and drop the metrics you want to see.
- Bookmark this page in your browser so you can access it easily.
- To go into more detail on campaigns, click on the campaign name. Doing this will take you to 'Ad sets' and 'Ad views', to compare the performance of individual audiences or specific ads.

RECOMMENDED COLUMNS FOR YOUR DASHBOARD
Campaign name. Delivery. Budget. Results. Reach. Impressions. Cost per result. Amount spent. Ends.

For metrics relevant to your Instagram page, choose: Post reactions. Post comments. Post saves. Post shares. Link clicks.

Once your dashboard is set up, see which ads and audiences generate which results. Sometimes engagement ads generate link clicks; sometimes link click ads generate engagement – they might surprise you.

Change the date range between lifetime, the last 30 days, the last 14 days and the last 7 days, so you can see if your ads are improving or decreasing in performance. If it's becoming more expensive to run the same ads, you might be experiencing audience fatigue or ad fatigue and it's time to mix one or both up.

ADVANCED
Add 'Conversions' to your dashboard and set up conversion tracking in Facebook Ads Manager, to measure downloads, purchases or registrations from your Instagram ads.

APPLY SMALL BOOSTS TO MULTIPLE POSTS WITH A DAILY BUDGET
Create an Instagram engagement funnel by applying small boosts to your feed posts using an ongoing campaign and a daily budget. This is one way to generate maximum results from minimal spending.

This method works to drive more engagement to your content, gather feedback on your posts and consistently put it in front of your target audience to grow your account.

1. Use Facebook's Ads Manager to set up an engagement campaign.
2. Don't select an end date and apply a daily budget of $2-4.
3. Choose the audience relating to your main target audience.
4. When prompted to create your ads, select 'Use existing post'.
5. Choose your six most recent posts, adding them as separate ads.
6. When you next post to your feed, visit Ads Manager, toggle the oldest ad off and follow the same process to add the new one.
7. Repeat every time you add a new feed post.

All of the engagement received via this method will show on your feed posts, undifferentiated from organic engagement.

Facebook's Ads Manager will split your daily budget across all of the ads, based on how they are performing, including their engagement rates. You will likely find that some ads outperform the rest and this will give you useful information to inform your future content.

Monitor the growth of your account and the engagement on each post via the ads dashboard you have set up. You can turn the entire campaign off at any point in your Ads Manager, then begin it again whenever you like.

4. Leverage geographical arbitrage to gain inexpensive likes

Some countries are more expensive to advertise within. Users in affluent countries have higher purchasing power, which means higher competition and Facebook's Ads Manager charging you more to reach them in terms of cost per click (CPC) and cost per thousand impressions (CPM).

Some of the most expensive countries to advertise within are the USA, UK, Norway, Germany and Sweden. On the other hand, targeting some countries can glean comparatively inexpensive CPC and CPM. This list varies depending on interests targeted.

If your product sells worldwide, or if your goal is to make your brand look bigger in terms of your Instagram followers or engagements, leveraging ad campaigns to less expensive countries is a legitimate way of growing your page versus purchasing likes or followers or using automated bots.

1. Use your Facebook Ads Manager to visit the Instagram engagement funnel you created in Rule 3 (see page 224).

2. At the 'Campaign' level, hover over the campaign name and select 'Duplicate'. This will replicate the campaign, ad sets and ads.

3. Rename this campaign to differentiate it, for example adding the word 'global'.

4. At the ads set level, create a new audience with the same interests, language, age and gender, but change the location of your audience.

5. Select 'Worldwide' and let Ads Manager work for you, or you could select specific countries based on research as to which offer lower ad targeting.

6. Keep adding new feed posts and toggling older ones off, as per your original campaign.

7. Test how these ads perform compared to those shown in your original campaign.

If you serve customers all over the world, continue to run this campaign alongside your original one that targets a more specific audience of your ideal customers.

If you don't offer products and services all over the world, then the followers and engagements gained using this method won't be as relevant to your brand. This approach should, therefore, be used as a short-term strategy, when you want to give a boost or initial spike.

If you serve customers from a specific location, use this method as part of a phased approach.

- ◀ Start by advertising these ads to 'Worldwide'.
- ◀ After a few weeks, narrow to your specific continent.
- ◀ Next, narrow to your country, then your city.

As the results become more expensive per click or per engagement, your page will have grown. Ads tend to perform better when the account or post already has a high level of followers and engagement, which is likely to counteract the increased cost of location targeting.

5. Test multiple posts, iterate campaigns

Facebook's Ads Manager is one of the only places you can advertise that doesn't let you spend your money on ineffective ads.

Imagine a billboard or TV advertising campaign. If you want to pay a billboard company to show an ad, they will likely let you put anything there; they don't have a vested interest in the ad succeeding. However, Instagram wants you to run ads that will be valuable to your target audience, because Instagram wants its users to enjoy their time on the platform.

Work with Facebook's Ads Manager to increase the impact of your ads, for the benefit of your brand. Go on a journey to reduce your cost per impression, link click or engagement.

TEST YOUR ADS

- ◀ **Run multiple ads within the same ad set.** For each one, make a small change and assess the results after you have enough data to spot trends.

- ◀ **Run the same ads to different audiences.** Make changes in location, demographics, interests and age ranges to see which glean better results.

- ◀ **See where Facebook is putting your budget.** Facebook will share your budget across ads, according to which are performing better.

Do the testing first and once you have a formula that works, ramp up the spending, if your budget allows. If you know that for every $2 you spend you make $10 of sales, it makes sense to add more budget to this campaign in an attempt to scale those numbers.

The best Instagram advertisers have carried out extensive testing. They know what works and they follow a formula for every new campaign. They are specific with their image or video composition, cover screen, image content and composition of copy, including the call to action. Their evidence is based on analysis of statistics, not anecdotal.

Become more proficient by making changes to the following specifics and assessing your performance.

- **Caption copy.** Reorder sentences to see if a different order is more effective. Use different copy entirely but keep everything else the same.

- **Call to action.** Test different phrases, buttons and link types but keep everything else the same.

- **Images.** Test the same copy and call to action, but use a different image for each ad. Test images of people versus products, smiling versus serious, different colour backgrounds or filters.

- **Video versus image.** Test your video ads versus your image ads, keeping the caption and call to action the same.

Change only one aspect of your ad at a time so you can be sure which change was responsible. Use all of this information to inform your photoshoots and organic content. Drop methods that don't work and focus efforts into those that do.

Measuring Results

There are many facets to your Instagram strategy and a lot of things might happen over the course of a week or a month. Your account might grow – but do you know why? What exactly is the source of the growth and what's the magnitude? Is this something you can scale? Measuring and recording your results is the only way you can truly assess your Instagram growth.

Of course, there are many cases of brands and individuals growing their accounts with a haphazard, happy-go-lucky approach, but that doesn't work for everyone. Sending high-quality content out into the ether and doing some active outreach on a regular basis should get you moving in the right direction, but if you're not keeping records, you're not learning. In reality, you could be growing your account faster or you could be doing it with half the effort. The key is knowing what is working and how well.

And if your account isn't growing as fast as you would like, without data you have to rely on your gut feeling or anecdotal evidence, or you have to go back over old content to figure out what's happening.

More than likes

Measuring results isn't just a case of seeing which posts perform best; it's about knowing how best to spend your time or marketing budget. Instagram activity doesn't happen in a vacuum, so it's important to look at the bigger picture in terms of return on investment. Certain insights may lead to a shift in focus or an overhaul of your strategy. You'll be able to quickly identify the fact you've plateaued, and you'll be in a better position to know how to get yourself out of it.

Keeping you on track

Knowing that you're tracking your progress towards your goals keeps you focused. It avoids you flitting around and changing course when you see what other individuals or brands are doing and feel tempted to try something out that isn't part of your plan. Consistent progress relies on you being intentional about all of your actions.

If you don't make records, you can't break records. If you're uncertain about how important all this measuring and analysis is, just look at the ocean of tools devoted to collecting this data and providing these insights. It's crucial.

Other benefits of measuring

Knowing your rate of progression allows you to predict your future account figures. Based on this, you may decide you need to increase your daily content, engagement activity or marketing spend.

It also gives you something to show to potential collaborators, customers or investors, depending on your business plan. If you decide to hand over the reins of your Instagram account to someone else, they'll have records and metrics to work with.

Note that in order to access the full suite of analytics on the platform, you will need a business account, which brands should have anyway. If not, you'll need to use third-party apps, but you may still find you're limited. Instagram's own insights are limited because insights cover the last seven days.

1. Monitor post performance

Alongside gathering general trends as to how your account is growing, scrutinise the information at an individual post level. Under each post, click 'Insights' to find the following basic data:

Likes: How many likes the post received.

Comments: How many comments the post received.

Send as message: How many accounts sent that post to another account, in a direct message.

Saves: How many accounts bookmarked your post.

Profile visits: How many accounts clicked to visit your Instagram profile directly from that specific post.

Reach: the number of unique accounts that viewed your post

Interactions: the total number of interactions with the post.

Even more interesting is this data:

The percentage of accounts reached that weren't already following you: How far the post went beyond your existing followers. Ideally, a large proportion of your reach came from people who weren't following you.

New followers: How many new followers you received directly from that post. This is likely to be higher if your content was seen by more non-followers.

Impression source: This shows where your post's impressions came from, split by home feed, hashtags, location or your profile. This breakdown will explain the success of your hashtagging, location tagging and algorithm-leveraging. The higher these numbers as a proportion of your follower number, the better.

Once you're familiar with the metrics, group your content into categories to find trends in performance. For example: group results for lifestyle shots, product shots, quotes or testimonial updates and videos. Look at the insights for one type of update and work out why some groups work better.

2. Instagram insights

As well as individual post insights, Instagram collects insights for your entire profile. Use the 'Insights' option to see information split by content, activity and audience. Here you can see:

◂ an overview of your activity: how often you shared and how many people saw your recent posts and stories

◂ the accounts reached in the past week, split by day and compared to the week before

◂ impressions in the last week and compared to the week before

◂ interactions in the last week and your most popular days

◂ profile visits and website clicks in the last week and compared to the week before

◂ audience details, including follows/unfollows, locations, ages, genders, and follower activity.

The data you see is for the last seven days only, so check it on the same day every week for the most useful data.

Each time you check Instagram's insights, ask the following questions:

1. What are the trends in my performance?

2. Does the output (results) match the input (time spent on platform, posts shared)?

3. Does my Instagram audience match that of my overall business and customer base?

4. How should I change my actions based on this data?

3. Using apps to gather more data

Use apps to gather more data on your Instagram activity. The best analytics apps will give you data further back than one week, as well as metrics that Instagram doesn't provide. They can also record and interpret the data better and some can be used on a desktop.

GOOGLE ANALYTICS
Use Google Analytics to assess your website traffic from Instagram and see if your followers are turning into website visitors and customers. From your Google Analytics dashboard, investigate the source of your traffic and see how many visitors arrived from Instagram. Track it over time and alongside any specific promotions.

ICONOSQUARE
Iconosquare takes a deep dive into your Instagram metrics and uses them to make recommendations, including when you should post content and stories. A 14-day free trial is available, then it's a monthly fee based on number of accounts and users.

SOCIALBAKERS
This platform has a free tool for Instagram statistics, designed to help you understand what your audience wants to see from your account.

UNIONMETRICS
A free Instagram checkup that pinpoints which hashtags you should use to get more engagement and what you should post more (or less) of.

SQUARELOVIN
This Instagram insights tool is free and gives monthly analytics on all of Instagram's metrics, including follower growth, post performance and engagement. There are insights on your communities' preferences and interests and advice on how to better drive engagement.

4. Keep records and make notes

Keep yourself and your team motivated by recording your personal bests (PBs) and celebrating when you set a new one.

Keep records of:

- most likes on one post
- most comments on one post
- most viewed story
- most sales from one post
- most DMs received from one story

... and any others of your choosing. For best results, write them down somewhere everyone can see them.

Think about what's important to your business and only record the metrics you actually care about and are actively focusing your efforts towards.

MEANINGFUL METRICS

- How many web visitors you've acquired from Instagram, recorded monthly. If appropriate, the number of signups, new users or sales from these visitors.
- Your entire month's reach, compared to the month before, to demonstrate effective use of hashtags and location tagging and the virality of your content.
- Your average number of likes and engagement on each post, to signal your content is resonating more with your audience.
- Data mapped to specific campaigns or activities, to assess the effectiveness of key pushes.
- How many posts and stories you shared in a month and how this affected the other metrics.

Record all this data in a spreadsheet and set yourself reminders to regularly fill it in.

5. Assess paid ads

When considering the effect of paid ads, as well as delving into the metrics for your campaigns, consider them as a whole and compare them to other outlays of time or money. Considerations should include:

ALTERNATIVE SPEND OF THE SAME BUDGET

Would the same budget be better spent elsewhere? Perhaps running a photoshoot to create better content that performs well organically? Perhaps hiring a copywriter to create captions that resonate with your audience?

TIME VERSUS MONEY

How much does every new like, comment or follower cost in advertising spend versus how much time it would take to amass the same via active outreach? Then determine the value of that person's time. This might mean their hourly rate, or what else they could achieve with the same time.

PERFORMANCE OF SALES ADS VERSUS GAINING CUSTOMERS ANOTHER WAY

Consider the various ways you attract new customers: word of mouth, referrals, networking and other advertising costs that perhaps include Google Ads. How do these compare to running Instagram ads? What is your cost per new customer via Instagram ads and is it lower via other means?

Paid ads might be a core part of your marketing efforts at different stages, but not suitable to run continuously. Your options are:

- ◄ run paid ads to reach certain follower milestones
- ◄ run paid ads for specific campaigns, launches or events
- ◄ run paid ads continuously, aiming to get more from the same budget.

Assess them compared to all other customer acquisition methods, but don't discount the benefits of having a large and engaged Instagram account in representing your brand.

6. Revisit your goals and strategy

Once you're running your Instagram with a consistent voice, active outreach and regular content that perfectly represents your brand, you can be critical of the goals created in Chapter One and assess how realistic they are.

Split your assessment into two sections:

1. Where are you making progress? What has caused the progress and how can you make even more progress?
2. Where are you wasting time? Which activities aren't yielding substantial results and which (if any) should you cut out?

Noticing the evolution of your account and the planned or surprise growth areas means you can check off some of your goals and set more relevant and ambitious ones.

EXERCISE Assess all of your activities against each other to work out what gives the best results per hour spent.

- ◀ Finding and speaking to new audiences versus talking directly to those already converted.
- ◀ Positioning your content to add value with sales as a byproduct, or vice versa.
- ◀ Being careful not to offend versus being provocative.
- ◀ Active engagement versus advertising.
- ◀ Following more people versus keeping your vanity ratio.

Assess whether setting these new goals results in a change in your overall strategy, or if you are already on the right path. Occasionally revising your goals is perfectly fine. Make sure you're working with the current version of your brand and your journey and let go of legacy goals that are no longer relevant.

TOP TIP Ramp up what's working. For example, if you know that motivational quote posts perform the best, drive the most engagement and generate the most new followers, produce them in bigger batches and share them more often.

Female Entrepreneur Association, UK

@FEMALEENTREPRENEURASSOCIATION

Carrie Green, Founder

The membership organisation focused on consistently serving its audience.

The Female Entrepreneur Association (FEA) exists to inspire and empower as many women as possible to turn their ideas into successful businesses. Its audience members are women from all over the world who are thinking about starting a business or are already building their own venture.

The Instagram account was opened in June 2017 and now has 108,000 engaged Instagram followers, many of whom are also members of FEA. Carrie shares how she built the account on a commitment to adding value.

CAN YOU TELL ME ABOUT YOUR INSTAGRAM GOALS?

At the start, our goal was to share inspiring and valuable posts that our audience would love. We knew if we could share content that aligned with the mission and values of FEA, we would attract the right people and build an audience that resonated with what FEA is all about.

Now that we have built a following, our goal is to grow it by continuing to share valuable and engaging content, but also to grow our email subscribers, drive traffic to our website and encourage our followers to become customers.

We constantly brainstorm creative ways to share offers in a way that engages our followers and encourages them to take action. Instagram stories have become a big part of this strategy because people can easily swipe up to find out more about what we're talking about. For example, to encourage our followers to become email subscribers we'll run a series of stories promoting a 'freebie' and give the call-to-action to 'swipe up' to download it. We do the same when promoting a product or service.

WHAT DO MEMBERS OF YOUR AUDIENCE HAVE IN COMMON?

Our audience members share doubts and fears, such as: 'I'm not good enough to do this!', 'I don't have the time!' and 'What if this fails?'. They also share many passions and goals, from being determined to quit their job to run their business full time, to building a million-dollar company and living the life of their dreams. The content we create cheers them on, truly speaks to where they're at and how they're feeling and encourages them to pursue their dreams. Having a clear understanding of our audience has been essential in building a community, not just a following.

HOW DO YOU ENGAGE WITH YOUR COMMUNITY?

We post once a day on our feed and we share multiple stories per day. We engage with our community by asking questions, chatting in the comments and utilising the features of Instagram stories, such as polls, questions and chat groups. Direct messages are also a powerful way we engage.

WHERE DOES YOUR INSPIRATION COME FROM?

We regularly survey our audience and ask them questions so we can tailor our content around their needs and desires. Our community members now cheer us on as much as we cheer them on. They share our content and often sing our praises. This reinforces the importance of using Instagram as a tool to serve, not as a place to take, take, take. It's about truly being there for your community and ensuring that being of service is your number one priority.

HOW HAVE SALES GROWN AS YOUR COMMUNITY HAS GROWN?

As our community has grown, we've been able to share our message with more people and as a result they want to be more involved with what we offer. They want more than to see our tips and posts on Instagram; they want more support, so naturally as our community has grown, sales have increased. We use tracking links to track sales, so we know how effective Instagram is for us.

CAN YOU EXPLAIN THE THINKING BEHIND YOUR PROFILE AND PICTURES?

We make sure everything we post has the FEA look and feel. From the colours and fonts, to the words we use, everything is well thought out before we share it to ensure it's a true reflection of our brand.

At the beginning we researched hashtags that would be good for our account and now we typically use them repeatedly. If we have a new type of post to share we'll definitely research new hashtags to use. We focus a lot on sharing inspirational quotes, which get really good engagement. People love seeing them and will often share with their own following. We also share our videos, podcasts and products.

Our account grows faster when we're 100 per cent consistent with posting. If we go through phases of not sharing as much, then engagement and growth noticeably slow down.

CAN YOU PREDICT HOW WELL A POST WILL DO BEFORE YOU POST IT?

We know that inspirational quotes will typically do better than us sharing a tip and we know that a video post will do better than a graphic with audio. Before we post something out we always ask ourselves, 'Would I stop and engage with this if I saw this from someone else in my feed?'. If the answer is no, we won't post it or we'll work on it until it's more compelling.

It's very hard to have ideas. It's very hard to put yourself out there, it's very hard to be vulnerable, but those people who do that are the dreamers, the thinkers and creators. *They are the magic people of the world.*

- AMY POEHLER

GET A MINDSET FOR SUCCESS!
Try these 4 amazing things!

THEY WANT MORE SUPPORT, SO NATURALLY AS OUR COMMUNITY HAS GROWN, SALES HAVE INCREASED. WE USE TRACKING LINKS TO TRACK SALES, SO WE KNOW HOW EFFECTIVE INSTAGRAM IS FOR US.

OUR ACCOUNT GROWS FASTER WHEN WE'RE 100 PER CENT CONSISTENT WITH POSTING. IF WE GO THROUGH PHASTES OF NOT SHARING AS MUCH, THEN ENGAGEMENT AND GROWTH NOTICEABLY SLOW DOWN.

Health

The effect of social media on our mental health is well documented. None of us is completely immune to the potentially harmful impact of spending too much time and energy on Instagram. Even if striving to have a purely commercial relationship with the platform, it's almost impossible not to let our emotions get involved.

The goal is to have all the benefits of Instagram without the negatives. We're winning when we leverage Instagram to grow our brand's influence. We're losing when we end up mindlessly scrolling the feed. It's essential to achieve production, not consumption, when it comes to social media.

Using technology to our advantage

Technology has the power to unite, removing many of the barriers that once existed between people from all over the world. However, social media can also be divisive. It creates an algorithm-driven echo chamber leading to insular and extreme views that are open to manipulation. Social media should be used to facilitate and enhance our real-world experiences, not replace them. These include:

- People buying and benefiting from your product
- People meeting you in real life
- Staying in touch to deepen relationships
- People visiting your shop or venue

Addictive by design

The popularity of social networks is no accident. Platforms like Facebook and Instagram are designed to be addictive. They are monetised through brands advertising to their users, so the greater the number of users and the longer they spend on their accounts, the more money the platforms stand to make.

Instagram employs an 'endless scroll' format, meaning users can keep scrolling posts as long as they want. According to the algorithm, as they go further and further into the archives, the posts should be of decreasing relevance to the user. However, if the urge is there, there is no shortage of content.

This feature also means that there's no natural end to the activity, as there would be when watching a film or reading a magazine. Therefore, Instagram can become a serious time and mental energy sponge without us realising. Opening the app and scrolling becomes a habit that we perform without even thinking about it.

The buzz that people get when they receive notifications on social media is a result of chemical changes in our brain. The 'happy' hormones dopamine and oxytocin are released in response to activities on social media, which make it so addictive. Our bodies crave those little buzzes and that's why we're so compelled to keep checking our the latest posts.

Mental health implications

A UK survey carried out by the BBC suggested that Instagram is rated as the worst social media platform when it comes to its impact on young people's mental health. 1,479 people aged 14–24 were asked to score apps on factors such as anxiety, depression, loneliness, bullying and body image.

FOMO (the 'fear of missing out') is a common form of anxiety caused by social media. If we see people having a great time while we're not there, this can create unhelpful thought patterns. This is the same for brands and businesses too. It's easy to feel that our brand isn't as successful as we'd like and we're missing out on things our competitors are doing.

Comparing our reality, both personal and business, to another account's edited feed rarely ends well. The insecurities we have are exacerbated, while we have little control over what other people get up to and what they post.

This section works through five valuable tips to avoid becoming drawn in by Instagram's addictiveness and the potential mental health issues associated with it.

1. Don't let Instagram monopolise your time

Stay in control of the time you spend on Instagram so that it doesn't monopolise your day. Approach your activity in a clinical way to make sure you get all the benefits without any of the downsides.

SET TIME LIMITS
Parkinson's Law states that tasks expand to fill the time made available for them. Before starting any Instagram activity, set a timer and stop when the time's up. You might be amazed at how productive you are.

SCHEDULE TIME AWAY FROM INSTAGRAM
Use Instagram's own 'time on Instagram' feature to monitor your daily usage and set limits. Be strict with yourself and resist the urge to use the override function.

BATCH ACTIVITIES
When you suddenly think of ideas for your Instagram, write them down. Only open Instagram when you have more than five written down and resist the urge to constantly open the app.

SIGNPOST ACTIVE HOURS
If you run an account designed for customer service, include your active hours in the bio. This way your audience knows when to expect a response and you don't need to check so frequently.

HIDE THE APP
Social media app icons are designed to be shiny and enticing. Keep your Instagram app off your home screen. Hide it away on the second screen or in a folder to ensure you use it deliberately not mindlessly.

PRODUCING OVER CONSUMING
Notice when you are are 'producing' content, engagement and ideas rather 'consuming' via scrolling and checking. Tip the balance in favour of producing.

2. Don't let Instagram affect your sleep

Late-night Instagramming is a recipe for a bad night's sleep. It's well documented that the blue light emitted by devices disturbs the natural production of melatonin, which controls the body's sleep cycles. Using your phone tricks your body into thinking it's time to be awake.

However, more than this and your brain will be awake with thoughts of content, ideas, metrics and the lives of the people you follow – all of which can wait until the morning.

To counteract this, create boundaries based on when you will carry out your Instagram activity.

- ◣ Set a cut-off time, at least an hour before your bedtime, when you will put your phone away.

- ◣ Don't Instagram in bed. Buy an alarm clock instead of using your phone's alarm and keep your phone out of reach of your bed entirely. You could charge it in a different room overnight.

- ◣ If you only use Instagram as part of your 9-to-5 role, consider using a separate phone that you leave at your place of work, so you're not tempted to work on it in the evening.

3. Remember your purpose

Social media can enhance someone's profile but rarely can it fabricate one from scratch. Not one of substance, anyway. Create an account of substance by committing to being exceptional in whatever it is that you do.

The most popular and well-loved Instagram accounts are those people and brands whose purpose is bigger than simply growing their Instagram accounts. They do something else really well. These accounts include world-class athletes, exciting brands, movie stars, entertainers and singers. Everyone is an artist honing their craft and the more they do this, the more it translates to Instagram success.

Your brand has a purpose. It might involve producing products that people love to use, providing a service that makes a difference or inspiring or motivating people into action by the example you set and the story you share. Focus on doing great work first and compel people into looking for you online. The more your customers love you, the more they will actively seek you out.

Keep Instagram in perspective by:

- defining the purpose of your work and prioritising it
- seeing your presence on Instagram as a fun and challenging game
- not taking anything personally (negative comments, unfollows, etc)
- remembering that behind every handle is a real person
- using it to promote and explain the work that you do, not replace it
- being the same person online as you are in real life
- treating everyone with kindness and respect.

4. Don't obsess over follower numbers

Your worth is not defined by the number of followers you have. Ensure that your mood or satisfaction is never tied to how well your latest post has been received. Quality counts for much more than quantity.

Focus on the inputs – the things you can control – and see everything else as playing a game. If your account isn't where you want it to be, it just means people haven't found you yet. Look at the bigger picture and keep perspective.

If you're a business to business (B2B) brand, only serving customers fitting a certain criteria, you might not naturally gather as many fans as a global customer-led brand would. Perhaps your account is relatively new. Don't compare the first few steps of your journey with established accounts that have been playing the game for longer. See them as inspiration showing what is possible and don't feel disheartened.

Focus on providing a service to your existing follower base, getting to know them and designing your content to surprise and delight them them and turn them into superfans. Chasing growth in favour of serving your existing network is a distraction. Serve your network well and the growth will happen.

If you have built a huge Instagram following that isn't translating into sales, realise that you've done the hard part. Take the next steps to work out what is missing and address it from the solid platform you've built. Turning Instagram into a valuable asset and not just a vanity platform takes consistency and is a long-term endeavour. The best view often comes after the hardest climb.

5. Stick to your own game

The more certain you are of your purpose, your goals and the route you will take to achieve them, the less you will worry about unhealthy comparisons.

Instagram is someone's carefully edited showreel. It's not their real life. Scrolling your home feed will inevitably result in seeing the milestones, travelogues and announcements of everyone you follow. Taking inspiration from other accounts and using it to explore new techniques or features to improve your own feed is good. Feeling happy for others without feeling envious is good. Comparisons that lead to insecurity, anxiety or sadness are not good.

Use the following steps to stick to your own game:

1. Regularly revisit your goals. Remind yourself of your progress and ensure you're working towards achievements that actually matter to you.

2. Be headstrong. As your account grows, you might start to receive advice on how you should post. Others might try to pull you in their direction for their benefit. Scrutinise carefully and say 'no' more than you say 'yes'.

3. Take the right steps for you. When you feel yourself becoming sidetracked by external opinions or influences, take a step back and reassess.

4. Don't take anything personally. Not everyone will like what you put out there, and that's fine. You don't need to impress everyone. Ignore any trolls because they aren't happy people.

5. Use only your former self as competition. Only compare your present to your own past and your own future.

Putting yourself or your brand out there on Instagram is a choice. You can opt out at any time. If it ceases to be what you want to do, you can log out, you can post less, you can make your account private, or you can outsource the activity to someone else. You have options. Those who win at the game are those who can take all the positives without internalising the negatives.

My favourite word is the Greek word 'euthymia'. From Seneca's essays, this translates as: 'Believing in yourself and trusting that you are on the right path, and not being in doubt by following the myriad footpaths of those wandering in every direction.'

I wish you a fulfilling and prosperous Instagram journey.

Final thoughts

It's nearly the end, and at the same time it's never the end.

Here's your challenge: to take everything you can from the 125 sections you've just read. To give them every chance of taking your brand on Instagram that little bit further. To take every single one of them seriously, discarding none. If it's made the book, it's made the difference to other accounts and there's no reason it can't for yours too.

Thank you for allowing me to guide you alongside your Instagram journey. I hope you are raring to go, equipped with all the knowledge and ideas and ready to absolutely smash it.

This book has showcased many incredible, yet varied, Instagram accounts. The one thing they have in common is that they all started at square one; with zero posts and zero followers. I hope this book has shown you that with enthusiasm and consistency, yours can be up there with the greats. I'm backing you to do this.

Stay on track throughout your Instagram journey and revisit the book when you need additional guidance, a new idea or a gentle reminder to persevere.

Finally, do keep in touch. I'd love to hear about anything you've changed or tried that led to amazing outcomes for your business. Feel free to message me on Instagram, Twitter or LinkedIn. You can also get in touch via my website jodiecook.com.

Wishing you success and happiness,

Jodie

Your exclusive invitation

Exclusively to Instagram Rules readers, you are invited to the JC Social Media Academy, containing hours of webinars and guidance on digital media, for further learning on Instagram, general social media and all other platforms.

Normally $99, signing up here will give you a 100 per cent coupon code. We'll also send you three bonus interviews with awesome Instagram accounts from which to learn.

Sign up at: jcsocialmedia.com/Instagram-rules

Index

Further reading

Never stop learning

Instagram has its own suite of tools for business owners complete with guidance and examples. Be inspired by more success stories and learn about new features as soon as they are available.

Find it at business.instagram.com

The JC Social Media blog has plenty of hints, tips and tricks for all aspects of digital marketing for business. It compiles the knowledge of the team and is perfect for those looking to expand their knowledge wider than Instagram.

Find it at jcsocialmedia.com/blog

For social media news and updates by marketing professionals from all over the world, you'll always learn something on Social Media Today. Worth bookmarking.

Find it at socialmediatoday.com

Instagram itself (of course) is on Instagram! These two accounts aim to demonstrate just what is possible with the platform, as well as give examples of new features. It's posting from:

@instagram and @instagramforbusiness

Acknowledgments

This book itself is proof that being visible online can bring incredible opportunities. There I was, minding my own business, when an email from Alice, commissioning editor at Quarto, arrived in my inbox with a request that I write the book she'd been planning. Thank you, Alice, for putting your trust in me to bring it to reality. I hope I have done it justice. Thanks for being awesome to work with.

Thank you to all of the team at Quarto whose vision and work have brought together such a beautiful and useful book. It looks better than I ever could have imagined and I'm excited for it to create huge success for millions of readers.

Thanks to the fantastic contributors who form part of this book, and the many others who shared their story. You didn't have to give such helpful and detailed answers, but you were each eager and willing to share the methods of your Instagram achievements so others can replicate them. It made all the difference and I'm very grateful to you.

Thank you to the team at JC Social Media for your endless ideas, creativity and exciting use of social media for our clients. Thanks for all being such a pleasure to work with.

A final thanks to my husband and #1 teammate Ben, for your help with every part of this book.

JODIE COOK is founder of JC Social Media, an award-winning team of social media managers and trainers based in the United Kingdom. The agency began in 2011 and has been representing clients across a changing social media world ever since, delivering social media management, training, online courses and a social media reporting tool.

Jodie writes books and articles on social media, entrepreneurship and happiness. These include *Stop Acting Like You're Going to Live Forever*, its accompanying guided journal, and a children's storybook series *Clever Tykes*, which gives entrepreneurial role models to 6-9-year-olds. You can find her writing at jodiecook.com/writer.

Jodie was included in *Forbes*' '30 under 30 social entrepreneurs in Europe 2017', and gave a TEDx talk with the title 'Creating Useful People'. She's a competitive powerlifter and loves to explore the world working remotely.

Find Jodie at jodiecook.com and on Instagram using @jodie.cook_

Brimming with creative inspiration, how-to projects, and useful information to enrich your everyday life, Quarto Knows is a favourite destination for those pursuing their interests and passions. Visit our site and dig deeper with our books into your area of interest: Quarto Creates, Quarto Cooks, Quarto Homes, Quarto Lives, Quarto Drives, Quarto Explores, Quarto Gifts, or Quarto Kids.

Instagram Rules
First published in 2020 by White Lion Publishing,
an imprint of The Quarto Group.
The Old Brewery, 6 Blundell Street
London, N7 9BH, United Kingdom
T (0)20 7700 6700 F (0)20 7700 8066
www.QuartoKnows.com

A catalogue record for this book is available from the British Library.

ISBN 978-0-7112-5176-2
10 9 8 7 6 5 4 3 2 1

Typeset in Saliec and Inka
Design by Nikki Ellis

Printed in China